For those who knew
and loved Evelyn Frey

LADY OF THE CANYON: EVELYN CECIL FREY

A TRIBUTE

BY

MARY D. BURCHILL

With COLLEEN OLINGER

OTOWI CROSSING PRESS
LOS ALAMOS, NEW MEXICO

Otowi Crossing Press
1350 Central Avenue
Los Alamos, New Mexico 87544

Library of Congress Catalog Card No.00-131038
Year 2001 Reprint 2007
ISBN 0-9645703-6-X
Paper

Edited by Colleen Olinger & Beverly Talley
Formatted by Ann Hamer, DownUnderWare
Cover design by Ann Hamer & Colleen Olinger

Contents

Illustrations

Foreword

When my husband and I came to Bandelier National Monument as seasonal rangers in the summer of 1995, we had a lot to learn. We spent the first summer reading almost everything that came our way about the park, the area, and the region. We went on ranger-guided walks, attended every campfire program, and listened to visiting speakers/scholars.

During our second summer, 1996, a long time former resident of the canyon, Mrs. Evelyn Frey, began to pique my interest. Who was this woman who had moved into the Frijoles Canyon, into an idyllic life but one that also had its problems? I read the snatches of information that were available about her from many different sources. Then I listened to her oral history tapes, which were made between 1979 and 1984 during programs called *Visits with Mrs. Frey*, and her personality began to emerge.

On our return in the spring of 1997 I knew *my* passion was to put her life in Frijoles Canyon into a form that others could read, learn from, and enjoy, while using her own words to bring out her personality and charm. Archaeologists tell us that people have lived in the canyon for possibly as much as 10,000 years. Could any of them have known it better or have loved it more than Evelyn Cecil Frey? I think not.

This is her story.

Preface

Evelyn Frey lived a very long life, one that spanned almost one hundred years (1892 to 1988). She was a pioneer—a frontier business woman who by-passed many of life's creature comforts to follow a passion that she may not even have recognized. She encountered, in her lovely canyon in northern New Mexico, the extremes of both nineteenth century rural isolation and twentieth century ecological tourism. She was a tenacious, self-supporting, single parent during a time when society judged these roles primarily in terms of failed relationships. She stubbornly lived her life according to her own code of integrity, responsibility, hard work, and courtesy.

Although she was a woman of intense personal privacy, Evelyn Frey allowed her late life reminiscences to be recorded by National Park Service rangers at Bandelier National Monument. The setting was a series of informal conversations with visitors occurring between the years 1979 and 1988. Her words from these taped *Visits with Mrs. Frey* form the backbone of this book. They are presented in italic lettering without footnotes. Evelyn Frey also participated in a few local public speaking events. Her words from these events are also presented in italic lettering, but with footnotes.

Through her own voice, Evelyn Cecil Frey has permitted us to view her life from <u>her</u> perspective, as <u>she</u> wanted it to be seen. She has provided, as well, rare insight into a unique culture that was subsumed by World War II, its modern cold war aftermath, and late twentieth century American society.

Acknowledgments

Even though this is a small book, there were many people who were instrumental in its coming together. Of course, many are associated with the National Park Service in general and Bandelier National Monument specifically. Chris Judson, ranger, alerted me to the tapes, constantly fed me information, and edited the first draft. Her suggestions were invaluable. Linda Gaffney, then manager of the Southwest Parks and Monuments bookstore in Bandelier, gave me insight into Evelyn Frey and kept encouraging me. Gary Roybal, the museum curator at Bandelier, was always gracious in making the archives available. Jane Walton, Evelyn Frey's half-sister, answered many questions and contributed information on the early years. Mary Sue Mills, a cousin of Mrs. Frey, had many memories and thoughts about Evelyn and her family which she shared with me.

Others who furnished information, support, and/or interviews were: Bob and Joanne Barnes, Romolo Cordero, Pamela Eckard, Reycita Garcia, Sally Hewitt, Dorothy Hoard, Elaine Jacobs, Thomas Krupp, Manuelito Martinez, Wil Martinez, Kevin McKibbin, Colleen and Bart Olinger, Virginia Salazar, Andrea Sharon, and Sari Stein

The Los Alamos Historical Society became very familiar to me; Hedy Dunn and Theresa Strottman were patient, interested, and helpful. I thank the Mesa Public Library in Los Alamos/White Rock for interlibrary loans and the alumni association of the New Mexico Military Institute in Roswell for furnishing information on Richard Frey. Barbara Stanislawski, museums curator for the National Park Service in Santa Fe, furnished pertinent information. Stark Brothers Nursery furnished me with a 1920 catalog, which allowed me to make a good guess as to the kinds of fruits brought into the canyon. The archives of the Los Alamos National Laboratory were also helpful. Ingrid Vollnhofer, librarian in the southwest collection of the New Mexico State Library, helped in person and answered questions by e-mail.

A grateful thanks are reserved to the rangers who did the oral tapes with Mrs. Frey: Chris Judson, Sari Stein, and Virginia Robicheau Salazar. The contributions of the tapes are never-ending.

A very special place in this whole process is reserved for Colleen Olinger, the publisher. She has a strong feeling for Mrs. Frey, and obviously you would not be reading this now if it were not for her. She has made the whole experience one which I will remember fondly.

But my biggest thanks go to my husband Brower. It was his knowledge of Bandelier that brought us here, his gentle encouragement that kept me going, his patience and faith that this could be done, and his great typing of the first draft. He recognized the importance of this project to me and to Bandelier.

This version of Evelyn Cecil Frey's life is mine as gleaned from the sources I used. Mistakes including deletions are mine also, but I'd be pleased and grateful to hear about additions or corrections.

Mary D. Burchill

June 2001

Adventure

Evelyn Cecil Frey

Take
the road
of high adventure

Search
for mysteries
yet unseen

Delve
into the unmet secrets
of this universe—
your house

Prove
that nothing is mysterious
when the natural laws
are known

Find
the source
of greatest knowledge
in the depths
of your own soul.

From "My last Christmas in Albuquerque, December 25, 1969"

1. The Beginning

A large canyon lies on the eastern slope of the Jemez Mountains in north central New Mexico. As the crow flies, it is about fifteen miles from Santa Fe; as the road goes, it is some forty miles away. Known by its rather prosaic Spanish name, Frijoles (Beans) Canyon, it is more than six hundred feet deep in places and forms a major impediment to north-south passage. A small stream, the tree-shaded Rito de los Frijoles, anchors Frijoles Canyon—flowing so far below the rim that the sound of its presence barely reaches onlookers at the top. Here in this huge land, humans are essentially alone.

Early in May 1925, a small three-member family paused before descending the steep canyon wall into a new life. George and Evelyn Frey and their ten-month-old son Richard were about to become the sole full-time inhabitants of the canyon floor so far below.

Under a soaring blue sky, the two adults unloaded their car—dishes, clothes, linens, household goods, fruit trees (mail-ordered by Evelyn from Stark Brothers Nursery in Missouri), and five hundred baby chicks. No road, not even a wagon road, wound into the canyon. Everything was strapped onto mules for the steep trek down. In later years, Evelyn Frey would recollect the trek this way,

I brought seventy-five fruit trees and . . . we got them on mules to bring them down, and . . . [the mules] bucked them off all the way down the trail. It tickled their rears and they'd just—here'd go the trees!

The trail the Freys followed from the rim down into the canyon was barely improved from the Indian path used by previous inhabitants or visitors. When Santa Fe's Judge Abbott came in 1908 to homestead, goods had to be unloaded from mules in some places, taken by hand down ladders to lower levels, and reloaded. The Freys, on the other hand, could travel the entire trail by mule without once unloading and reloading.

1

If Frijoles Canyon was isolated within its immediate landscape, it was even more isolated from the surrounding world. It is doubtful that George and Evelyn Frey could have traveled by car the entire one-hundred-mile distance from their home in Albuquerque in even a day. The road from Albuquerque through Santa Fe to Pojoaque, the closest tiny settlement to the Jemez Mountains, was improved but certainly not paved. La Bajada hill, a steep escarpment south of Santa Fe, was the first obstacle. In the 1920s the road over La Bajada consisted of a series of treacherous, steep switchbacks which forced many cars to back up it in reverse, a car's most powerful gear. Over the years the road, now I-25, has moved to the east and today the grade is hardly noticeable.

Travelers to Frijoles Canyon in 1925 turned west at Pojoaque, some fifteen miles north of Santa Fe. The last twenty-five miles of the trip took them toward the mountain plateau, past San Ildefonso Indian Pueblo, on a "road" that was often mere ruts. The road followed the Pojoaque wash, the sandy bottom of a once-in-awhile river.

When the wash was dry the way was fairly decent; after a thunderstorm it could become impassable.Summer storms occasionally sent torrents of water down dry arroyos. Even after the run-off passed, mud often posed other hazards. Getting stuck or breaking an axle was as common along the Pojoaque road as to be almost expected. Folks in trouble camped until help arrived in the form of fellow travelers.

Vehicles crossed the Rio Grande on the new plank bridge at Otowi Crossing. The Chile Line, a narrow-gauge branch of the Denver and Rio Grande Western railroad track running from Colorado through Española to Santa Fe, crossed the river here on a trestle. The trestle also served cars and trucks for three years from 1921, when Buckman Bridge (two miles downstream) totally washed out, until 1924, when a narrow new bridge was completed north of the trestle.

The road continued south and west of the Rio Grande toward Pajarito Canyon, a couple of miles distant, and then on the old Buckman sawmill road up-canyon before climbing to the mesa top. This climb out had an almost impossible eighteen percent grade and was known as the Devil's Slide. Many years later, during a talk to the Los Alamos Historical Society, Evelyn Frey described the extra effort this section of the road caused travelers.

When we were too heavily loaded, we'd have to stop at the bottom [of the Devil's Slide] and take a lot of things out of the truck, take some up to the top, and come back and do this again.[1]

From the Devil's Slide, the road traveled west along the mesas some eight miles until it reached the sawmill area, here branching south to Frijoles Canyon and west into the Jemez Mountains. The trip was tough. On a good day a traveler leaving Santa Fe in the morning might, at the earliest, reach Frijoles Canyon by mid afternoon.

When the Frey family descended into Frijoles Canyon that bright May day in 1925, they were entering but one canyon of the Pajarito Plateau, the rugged landform that skirts the eastern side of the Jemez Mountains. Formed from hardened volcanic dust called tuff, the plateau comprises a landscape unique to itself. Perhaps the clearest general description of the region comes from the pen of turn-of-the-century newspaperman and writer Charles Lummis in his 1893 classic book, *The Land of Poco Tiempo.*

The Cochiti upland [Pajarito Plateau] is a vast and singular plateau in the centre of northern New Mexico, some fifty miles west of Santa Fe. Its average altitude is over seven thousand feet; and along the west it upheaves into the fine Valles range of eleven thousand. Between these peaks and the Rio Grande, a distance of twenty miles, lies the plateau proper—a vast bench approximately level to the eye, furred with forests and peculiarly digitated with canyons. . . . Perhaps the best idea of its ground-plan is to be had by laying the two hands side by side upon a table, with every finger spread to its widest. The Rio Grande flows about north and south through the line of the knuckles. . . . The spread fingers represent the canyons, the wedge-shaped spaces between them are the tall potreras [mesas].[2]

Frijoles Canyon is one of two major canyons on the Pajarito Plateau containing year-round stream flow. It is seventeen miles long, about a quarter of a mile across at its widest, and some six hundred feet deep. The Rito de los Frijoles threads its entire length and empties into the Rio Grande.

Humans have been in and around the Frijoles and its sister canyons for perhaps ten thousand years. Both Cochiti and San Ildefonso Indian pueblos claim that their homes in Frijoles Canyon predate Spanish homes. Even though Native Americans left before the Spaniards came, they briefly reoccupied the canyon during the pueblo revolt of the late 1600s.

In 1740 Captain Andres Montoya sued the Spanish government for a grant to the land that included Frijoles Canyon. The Montoya family, including in-laws, farmed or grazed the land until the early 1800s. Spanish authorities ordered residents briefly out of the area in 1811 because they could not be protected from outlaws headquartered on the plateau. During most of the nineteenth century, the area continued to be used primarily for grazing by both Hispanic and non-Hispanic owners or lease-holders.

In the late 1890s an Oregon lumberman, Henry Buckman, bought the timber rights to much of the Pajarito Plateau north of Frijoles Canyon from then owners George N. Fletcher and Winfield R. Smith. Buckman created the small railroad shipping station of Buckman on the east bank of the Rio Grande. He built a makeshift bridge over the river and constructed a road to his sawmill on the mesa northwest of Frijoles Canyon.

The canyon became part of Bland District in the new Jemez National Forest in 1905. In 1906 the United States Forest Service stationed Albert Abbott of Santa Fe in Bland District as a forest guard. During Abbott's tenure in the district, John and Cyrus Dixon, graduates of Carlisle Indian School and probably residents of Cochiti Pueblo, took him to Frijoles Canyon to see their ancestral home. The men came into the canyon over the south rim on a very bad and neglected trail and stayed overnight in the remains of an adobe house. Abbott marveled at the numerous prehistoric cliff dwellings in the canyon.

Forest Service officers were always on the lookout for possible administrative sites and Abbott recognized that Frijoles Canyon, with its year-round stream, abundant vegetation, and historic value, was ideal. He sent a report to his supervisor in Santa Fe recommending the canyon as a new Forest Service site. At the same time he wrote his father, Judge A.J. Abbott of Santa Fe, about what he had seen.

A year later Judge Abbott, then in his seventies, and his new wife Ida viewed the canyon and contracted with the Forest Service to lease it and become its custodians the following spring. Judge Abbott arranged for the Forest Service to build a home for him and Ida. The Forest Service also built a road to the canyon's north rim from the Buckman road. From there the Abbotts packed everything down an old Indian trail.

The remains of a large prehistoric community house called Tyuonyi dominated the canyon floor. The formidable southwestern archaeologist Edgar L. Hewett oversaw excavations at Tyuonyi from 1908 through 1912. Many scientists who later became famous cut their archaeological teeth at Tyuonyi and other Frijoles Canyon sites. Judge Abbott and Ida contracted to provide meals for the workers. According to one of the excavators, Neil Judd, "The three pancakes which we workingmen were allowed at the Abbott breakfast were undeniably the thinnest pancakes ever served in New Mexico."[3]

Already Frijoles Canyon was an exotic destination for Santa Fe tourists on a day's outing to the Pajarito Plateau, where Tyuonyi was the primary attraction. Judge Abbott and Ida provided room and board for the tourists. They named their home Ranch of the Ten Elders because of the great number of box-elder trees growing beside the Rito de los Frijoles. For building material the Abbotts used prehistoric tuff building blocks from Tyuonyi. They ran their business, entertained family, and seemed happy in their idyllic setting.

From before the turn of the century, Edgar Hewett had lobbied for a national archaeological preserve that would have encompassed much of the Pajarito Plateau. However, neighboring Santa Clara Indians and local homesteaders, ranchers, and lumbermen opposed such a large withdrawal of public land. On February 11, 1916, President

Woodrow Wilson proclaimed the much smaller 22,400 acre southern portion lying within the Santa Fe National Forest, which included Frijoles Canyon, as Bandelier National Monument. The monument was named after ethnologist Adolph Bandelier, who had visited and reported on Frijoles Canyon in 1880, and remained under the administration of the Forest Service.

In 1919 when Judge Abbott was eighty-two years old, the Abbotts moved on. Between the years 1919 and 1925, three families lived in the canyon—the Boyds, the Reeds, and the Davenports. John and Richard Boyd took over the Abbott lease and lodge. In 1923 the Boyds deeded the lodge to Robert J. Reed who, with J.E. Davenport, continued to run it as a year-round resort called Frijoles Canyon Lodge. The address was Buckman, New Mexico.

During the 1920s the land north of Frijoles Canyon was occupied by the Los Alamos Ranch School, the Frank Bond family of Española—who used its property as pastureland, and various mostly Hispanic homesteaders. Cochiti Indian Pueblo was the largest neighbor to the south.

Evelyn Cecil Frey was thirty-three years old when she began life in isolated Frijoles Canyon. At slightly more than five feet tall with auburn hair and bangs, she was hardly a figure to draw attention. She was not considered beautiful or handsome. A friend, George Maoru, would later describe her,

> Well, she was a very modest dresser. She usually wore a dress or a skirt, and she wore a hat—nothing fancy. It was very nice; [she wore] pretty, well-kept clothes. You know, she was a very slight woman . . . and her skin was very pale. She wasn't one that got out in the sun, didn't give the idea of an outdoor person.[4]

She was born Evelyn Lenora Cecil in Vanderwoort, Arkansas, February 12, 1892, to Alfred Richard Packard Cecil (A.R.) and his wife Sarah. When Evelyn was about seven, her father moved the family to

New Mexico in an effort to cure Sarah of tuberculosis—a fairly common practice at the time. Evelyn's two younger brothers, Hubert and Jack, were born in New Mexico when she was in her early teens.

A.R. took his family to the tiny settlement of Pines in the southern Jemez Mountains thirty miles west of Santa Fe. He operated a sawmill there, shipping the lumber by rail from Buckman to a mill in Louisiana. Pines was some six miles from the booming mining town of Bland, then in its heyday. Begun in 1894 as a silver mining camp Bland grew quickly; by the early 1900s the town held three thousand people in its sixty-foot-wide canyon. Typical of frontier mining boom and bust, its energy was short-lived. By 1906 Bland was a ghost town.

I guess you'd call it a rip-snorting settlement at one time because my father said when it closed, it closed all at once. He said in this little narrow space in the canyon there were twenty six saloons.

Life for a frontier child, even under normal circumstances, was not carefree. It was probably especially rigorous for Evelyn—the oldest child and only daughter, who also had an ailing mother. Evelyn must have assumed major responsibility for household chores—cooking, sewing, washing, cleaning, care of the boys. She certainly knew daily work and the rewards of completing a job while doing it as best she could. No doubt she knew the frustration of having to do a job over until it was done right. Although frontier life was not easy or totally enjoyable, it gave her a life-long love of the outdoors and an appreciation for hard work.

Summers were spent in the mountains. During the school season Evelyn and later the two boys, when they were old enough, were sent to St. Vincent of the Sisters of Charity, a Catholic school in Albuquerque. In addition to regular schoolwork, Evelyn learned the social graces and how to sew, embroider very nicely, and play the piano—not well, she said, but it was what young ladies did. At one time or another during her life, she indicated that boarding school was not a great experience for her. And even though she spent her school years with nuns, she was not a religious person in the sense of attending church. (Nevertheless, many of those who later knew her commented on her spirituality, on her belief that a larger force guided the world.)

Evelyn was twenty-three years old when her mother Sarah died in 1915 at the age of forty-one.

She was so wonderful. . . . The last thing she ever said to me was, 'Evelyn, watch the little boys.'

Hubert and Jack were nine and eleven when their mother died and Evelyn became the woman of the house. The boys had lived some with relatives, but it appears they were now all together without their mother. A.R. moved his family to central New Mexico either shortly before or after his wife's death. He ranched and ran a small general store about twenty-five miles from Encino, where their post office was located.

We were truly isolated but in a perfectly exquisite place. It was a stage stop between . . . Denver and Texas. The little boys were small. They'd dig out in the yard once in a while and come in with a nickel or penny or something. Somebody dropped some money, don't you see?

In 1917 A.R. married Orofina Young, previously of Missouri. Orofina was the widow of a man who, like Sarah, had come to new Mexico to seek a cure for tuberculosis. While Evelyn thought well of her father's new wife, she remembered the sudden increase in family size as a mixed blessing.

She brought her mother and her son and herself and there were four of us, so I found I was doing the cooking for the family all the time.

A daughter Jane was born soon after A.R. remarried. In her last years Evelyn would claim Jane as her only close relative.

Evelyn met her future husband, George Xavier Frey, in Albuquerque. Born and raised in Oklahoma, he was two years her senior. His father

Henry owned an Oldsmobile car dealership and George was working for him as a mechanic. According to Evelyn, George had been chief mechanic for famed car racer Eddie Rickenbacker, which gave him the opportunity to travel.

> *And that's the kind of life that George liked . . . and if there ever was a country person, it's me.*

George and Evelyn Frey were wed November 8, 1917, in the tiny town of Palma in central New Mexico. Evelyn was twenty-five, George twenty-seven. It appears that for Evelyn the decision to marry was not clear cut.

> *I didn't know Mr. Frey a good long time, but I didn't want . . . . I never wanted to marry. I married him.*

The Freys set up house in Encino. George became proprietor and manager of an auto repair business. His stationery letterhead proudly proclamed, "Expert Automobile Repair." In August 1918 during the United States' participation in World War I, George enlisted in the army. He mustered out as a private in December after the war's end. The couple moved to Roswell in southeastern New Mexico, probably because of better business opportunities in the larger town.

Meanwhile Henry Frey had entered the shipping business and was spending time in Tampico, Mexico. He asked George to work for him overseeing his machinery. In 1921 Evelyn obtained a passport and traveled with George to coastal Lousiana, where the elder Frey was repairing a recently purchased one-hundred-foot-long freighter, the *Venus*. A captain on the scene convinced Evelyn that the ship was unsafe and advised her to "go home to daddy." Evelyn remained behind and George went on alone to Tampico. Evelyn followed a few weeks later on a separate freighter.

George and Evelyn stayed two years in Tampico. She nursed some and he worked in the oil fields. Mexico was a free and open place where anything could happen. Evelyn saw robbers, gunfighters, and desperadoes and she journeyed to wild Vera Cruz. During this time, however, the

9

Freys experienced their first joint tragedy. The *Venus* foundered while on a Gulf of Mexico crossing, losing all hands including George's father. The sole remnants of the ship were two or three fuel barrels. Soon the couple returned to Albuquerque.

George and Evelyn's only child, Richard George Xavier, was born in Albuquerque July 10, 1924. Shortly before or after Richard's birth, the idea of moving into Frijoles Canyon probably entered Evelyn's mind. Perhaps her father had heard of the lodge's availability or perhaps Sarah Reed, a school friend with family ties to the canyon, brought it to her attention. It is quite clear that Evelyn was the force moving the family forward.

> *I made the decision; Mr. Frey didn't. . . .The country didn't appeal to him like it did to me because I'd always been in the country. . . . My grandfather was a horticulturist. I have to farm.*

2. Business in Frijoles Canyon

George, Evelyn, and Richard Frey, in that spring of 1925, found the canyon buildings little changed from Judge Abbott's day. The living room was about the size of today's gift shop at Bandelier, approximately twenty by thirty feet; the floors were wooden. There was no running water and certainly no indoor bathroom. Cooking was done on a wood-burning stove. Several detached cabins housed visitors.

Up the canyon about a mile, the Forest Service ranger, or custodian, had his cabin. He was there only in the summer. The ranger's main job was to greet guests when they came down the trail, tell them what there was to see, and sometimes even take them on a tour. Then he would wait for the next group to come. In "off" times he looked after the trails and generally kept the park in working order. Occasionally Evelyn would be called on to tell visitors what was in the canyon. At first she knew little about the archaeological cliff dwellings and artifacts.

I had an idea. I asked our senator to send me a catalog on the Bureau of Ethnology, and he sent me eighty-nine volumes. So I set myself down of an evening and informed myself a little bit, and then when we had someone come in and no one to take them, I could.

Evelyn bought "unbleached domestic" (muslin cloth) at ten cents a yard and made curtains for the lodge and cabins. She painted a mother turkey followed by several little turkeys along the bottom of the curtains. Susie Davenport Reed, Robert's wife, was the person who reportedly first copied a turkey symbol from petroglyphs on the canyon cliffs and adapted it for use on curtains in the earlier lodge. But Evelyn claimed she refined it into what we see today. She used the symbol on dishes in the lodge and on lodge stationery, always associating herself with its origin.

It is a symbol that I got off the cliffs up here, but I worked the tail over there a little bit.

The symbol is now an unofficial National Park Service and concessionaire logo for Bandelier National Monument.

After getting settled, one of the family's first chores was planting the fruit trees in the small orchard remaining from the Abbotts. Based on a viewing of a 1920 Stark Brothers catalog, we can surmise that the new plantings may have included Red Delicious, Golden Delicious, Grimes Golden, and Jonathan apples; Elberta and J.H. Hale peaches; Gold America and Omaha plums; Superb apricots; Anjou, Duchess, Keifer, and Gold Nugget pears; Montmorency cherries; and Cumberland raspberries.

Evelyn and George sited the garden and orchard near the ruins north of the Rito de los Frijoles. May 1925 was rather dry, with only an inch of rain. Carrying water to seventy-five trees was time consuming, even if assisted by hired help, so George needed to work on an irrigation system right away. His system was rudimentary at first. He cut down a big pine tree in the canyon, hollowed it out, and used it as a flume—a time-tested Hispanic practice in northern New Mexico.

We had the only irrigation ditch here in the river. We piped it across an arroyo [using] a big pine tree, and it was hollowed out, and we used that as a flume across an arroyo there. . . . Every two feet there was a hole and you could stop this up. And we'd run it the whole [way along the garden].

Later George replaced this system with a concrete ditch that carried water from the Rito de los Frijoles to their two and one-half acre garden and orchard. It probably took seven to eight years before the orchard began to produce in quantity. During that time, small fruits—raspberries, blackberries, and strawberries—kept the canyon community in pies, jams, and jellies. These were supplemented with wild-growing strawberries, currants, gooseberries, and chokecherries. The strawberries were especially abundant.

[We had] a strawberry bed which was an alarming thing during the ripening season. Great big wonderful strawberries!

The Freys constructed none of the visitor cabins at the lodge. Evelyn thought that Judge Abbott had built them all, five or six stone structures up-slope and up-canyon a little from the main lodge building. Tradition, unproven, holds that Frank Lloyd Wright designed the cabins and that Carlos Vierra, an artist from Santa Fe, designed the fireplaces.

The cabins were not modern in any way. Fireplaces provided the only heat, and water had to be carried to all the rooms. A pitcher of water sat in a big bowl in every cabin. To wash, guests poured water from the pitcher into the bowl and afterward threw the used water out the door. The "facilities" (privies) were "up the hill."

> We had the most beautiful privy you have ever seen. It was built of rock and [had] a beautiful bench, or what you call it, with a high one, a low one, and a little one.

George dug a well and cistern, which allowed him to "modernize" the kitchen with running water and install two public bathrooms—one for ladies, one for gentlemen. He also put in a laundry and linen storage area. Another welcome addition was a drinking fountain.

> We dammed the little river and it had a sand filter. And our water was beautifully clear and as soft as it could be. I loved that water. Now it's different. It doesn't taste right to me.

The Freys had water rights to the Rito de los Frijoles. Under New Mexico water law, they could use creek water for irrigation. Eventually, in 1942, Evelyn got around to paying a $1.00 fee to change the rights from A.J. Abbott to herself.

> I had the rights to the river, and I was told I was the only one in the United States who had river rights.

The lodge could house about twenty guests overnight. There was also overnight camping. In addition many people came just for the day despite the fact that the trail in and out was far from easy. The writer

Charles Lummis, who had come into the canyon at least once with Adolph Bandelier and considered the canyon as spritually his own, insisted on staying in the caves when he visited.

> *Mr. Frey would begin to swear [when] . . . Mr. Lummis would say that he was coming out to stay with us awhile. He had a cave, and we had to take a cot and bedding and a wash bowl and pitcher during those days and a potty and everything you could think of over there, and he lived in the cave rather than coming over and having meals with us.*

Frijoles Canyon was both home and business for the Freys. Aside from their token Forest Service lease, they paid no rent to anyone and relied on their own perseverance to make ends meet. The only fiscal information available is from three years federal tax receipts located in the Bandelier National Monument archives. In 1924, before the Freys' arrival, the Frijoles Canyon Lodge income was $975.31. The partners were R. J. Reed and J. E. Davenport. In 1925 the income was $565.77. The partners were now George X. Frey and J. E. Davenport. The 1926 income was $726.11, with George X. Frey as sole owner.

Providing consistently good food for a varying number of people day in and day out was a challenge. Because they were isolated, Evelyn and George had to plan ahead. They bought flour, coffee, and sugar staples during infrequent, difficult trips to Santa Fe. Forgetting any of these was not good. Once, according to Evelyn,

> *Neither of us had bought coffee, so he [said] to me, 'Can't you think of something that you could make coffee out of? Do something.' . . . And I think I put a little molasses in hot water, and maybe food coloring, and I don't know what all I did. So after we got through with that he said, 'Evelyn, please don't make any more coffee.' And in a little while we got into town and got our coffee.*

Guests arriving at the canyon rim would phone down to the lodge, requesting horses for the trip into the canyon. As the visitors passed Bear Rock on the trail, the Frey's chef counted them; then meal preparations could begin. Food was central to the operation of the lodge and was often what was longest remembered by the guests.

A woman [once] said to me, 'I want to ask you something. Would you please tell me what you fed my husband forty one years ago?' I said, 'Lady, you wouldn't ask me that, please.' 'Yes' she said, 'I want you to tell me because,' she said, 'every now and then he'll say, 'Well, I remember Mrs. Frey's lunches being so good.'

Chicken, almost always fried and served with biscuits and milk gravy, was a summer staple.

The chef would butcher the chickens and put them in a great jar or a crock of salted water overnight, and the next morning he washed them and drained them. It was mighty good chicken.

Vegetables such as peas, beans, or corn came fresh from the garden. Bread was baked as needed—eight to ten loaves at least every other day, daily if necessary. The fresh bread was a special hit with guests.

I recall one man, I asked him if he'd have dessert and he said, might he [just] have another slice of bread or two and some homemade butter!

Raspberry pie was a favorite dessert. Ice cream was another favorite. The chef made it from cream, eggs, sugar, and vanilla or garden-fresh fruit flavoring. He obtained the ice to freeze the ice cream from an ice storage shed that George built.

[In winter Mr. Frey] dammed off the little river down here way up and . . . it would freeze, and then he'd flood it and it'd freeze [again]; it'd get about this thick. So he built a little ice house and insulated it with sawdust.

The sawdust was available in large quanities from abandoned sawmills north of the canyon.

In the summer Evelyn canned garden and orchard produce for eating in the winter. She and the chef put up jars of peaches, crocks of kraut, big pimiento peppers, pickles, and some vegetables. Other vegetables were stored underground.

Cabbages, . . . you'd dig a trench and you'd put the heads of the cabbage down in. You'd cover it all over and leave the stems sticking out. So we did that and, until the ground would get too frozen, just lift up a big head of cabbage [when we needed it].

If fruit harvests were abundant, Evelyn and George passed along some of the harvest to the Los Alamos Ranch School and homesteaders on the mesas.

When I had too much fruit, I shared my fruit with the neighbors. . . . They were mighty nice people.

Meals at the lodge were cooked on a wood-burning range that the Freys had brought in either by horseback or on a "sled," a wagon box without wheels that slid on the ground as it was pulled by a horse or mule. Baking was done in the oven of the same stove. Heat regulation on a wood stove was nearly impossible, so cooking several different items at varying temperatures and having them come out right and on time was an art. Meals were served family style in the dining room or on the porch (portal).

Our living room was tremendous and then we had a long portal. I know Mr. Frey said it was forty eight foot long and sixteen foot wide, and we served from our kitchen out into the patio—it was screened.

Evelyn always had a chef during the busy summer months. One special chef worked for her for nine years.

He was a Frenchman—very wonderful gentleman. Educated. . . . He [had] considered being a hobo the very finest job that anyone could ever have when he was a young man, and when he was older, he said he'd still like to just be a hobo.

16

This man (whose name is not recorded in Evelyn Frey's or Bandelier National Monument's records) had a drinking problem, a fault apparently held in common with most of her chefs.

I told him one summer when we closed, I said, 'You know, I don't believe I'm going to bring you back, chef, because you have been drinking all summer.' And I was doing most of the cooking and I was getting tired of it. So in the spring time I received a little message from him, and he said, 'Mrs. Frey, it is time to plant the onions.' So we wired him a ticket and he came home and stayed with us.

When he died, the Freys saw to his burial.

George and Evelyn raised cattle, pigs, and chickens. Turkey and deer meat came from the wild. They kept several cows to provide milk, cream, butter, and cottage cheese.

We had cows, too, which I had to milk. No one could milk. [Actually,] I think they could, but they didn't want to.

Gardening, harvesting, cooking, cleaning, caring for stock and guests— all these tasks were accomplished by Evelyn and George, a housekeeper, a chef, an occasional dishwasher, and one outside workman. George was not a farmer, but he contributed immensely to the workings of their canyon farm. He built stock bridges, put in irrigation systems, took care of the animals, repaired buildings and fences, hunted, butchered—all in a day's work.

Perhaps George's greatest achievement was installing a cable system from the north rim of the canyon down to the canyon floor. With this, life was easier because everything entering the canyon did not have to be carried down the trail. It is not clear when the cable was built. According to Evelyn they had been in Frijoles Canyon five or six years when George brought a Dodge pickup piecemeal into the canyon via the cable in bigger pieces than could be brought down on the trail.

The cable was eleven hundred feet long and had a vertical drop of about six hundred feet to the canyon floor. It had a basket or box in which to haul items and could be powered from either the top or bottom by one of two gasoline motors, one at each end. its uses were many. Cargos included linens sent out to be washed, luggage, firewood, and store-bought staples

Although many people visited the southwest, it was the Harvey Indian Detours that marketed and opened the area to large-scale travel. The Fred Harvey Company initiated Harvey Detours to complement their success with restaurants and hotels along the Atchison, Topeka and Santa Fe Railroad. The company purchased Koshare Tours of Santa Fe from writer Erna Fergusson in 1926 and hired her to train their guides, called couriers. Fergusson had used guides like this very successfully on her tours and had visited Bandelier several times.

The Harvey Company was headquartered in Santa Fe's La Fonda Hotel. From there tourists could take tours to local Indian villages and other attractions. Two Harvey employees accompanied each tour. One was the driver, a handsome young man in western clothes and a ten-gallon hat. The other was the courier, an attractive young lady wearing a western skirt and blouse and Indian jewelry. The couriers exuded an air of sophistication.

They were such beautiful girls. Their business was to see that the guest was taken care of properly, that you had the proper things to eat and a proper place to sleep.

The Harvey Detours were usually in and out in a day, returning to the La Fonda at night. Large Packard touring cars with high wheels allowed the tours to successfully travel the often miserable roads. Tours arrived at Frijoles Canyon several times a week during the summer.

I remember one time we had sixteen or seventeen cars at one time. It was a large tour. They would phone down and the chef would swear . . . [and] we'd get started on lunch.

The tourists had to leave the cars and walk or ride horses down the trail.

I recall one driver that—it's a disease, but I don't know what you call it—he had to walk on the outside of the trail to keep this man from jumping off his horse over the cliff. And then going back out, he had to do the same thing. . . . The boys and girls would once in awhile get in the basket and go ride out the cable, but they weren't supposed to do that. But they'd ride it anyhow, because climbing that trail . . . you'd literally fly down but going back is quite an effort.

Harvey Houses had reputations as well-run, nicely appointed hotels with first-class, fine restaurants. Evelyn considered it a compliment to be compared to them.

[Someone would say,] 'Oh, this is a Harvey House; just look!' I'd puff up.

Bandelier National Monument's archives contain several guest registers from the Frey days. Many visitors came from Santa Fe. Others came from Chicago, Detroit, Denver, New Jersey, Cleveland, Switzerland, New York, Kansas, all over. (See Appendix A.) One of the best-known visitors was Willa Cather.

And then Willa Cather was with us, I think around ten days when she was writing Death Comes to the Archbishop. She [was] a very pleasant, sort of middle aged, [woman]. I think she was never married. A quiet woman and we liked her so much. She was getting material or writing the things mostly that she had together here when she was working on that book.

For some reason, probably word-of-mouth advertising, doctors at Bellevue Hospital in New York City started coming to Frijoles Canyon for week-long stays. One such doctor would leave his wife at Bishop's Lodge in Santa Fe. He'd sit in a rocking chair at the end of the veranda, instructing Evelyn that he wanted to rest and was not to be disturbed. Another doctor asked to help in the kitchen.

'May I have breakfast in the kitchen with the family?' I said, 'You just come right in.' So he stayed with us about two weeks—picked and canned peaches with the chef. When he got ready to go away (he was a very wonderful person) he said, 'You know, Mrs. Frey, I'm a new man.'

The Freys advertised very little. Evelyn sometimes ran ads in newspapers or placed brochures at hotels; sometimes they received an occasional mention in a magazine article. Most of their trade seemed to result from word-of-mouth praise.

Their hotel rates were reasonable. In old age Evelyn remembered them as $2.50 a night , which may have included a meal or two. A meal cost twenty-five cents. This compared with a steep $80.00 a week at Ghost Ranch near Abiquiu, New Mexico—a price, however, which included everything, even extra pack trips and excursions.

The Freys remained in the canyon all winter. They were usually very much alone because the rangers came only for the summer months and moved out in September. Infrequently, visitors might arrive,very chilled, and stay a week or two. Fireplaces provided the only heat in all the cabins.

We had this big, big fireplace in our living room. We'd make a big, big fire and they'd sleep all over the floor. We'd have a little mattress or something [for each one].

Obtaining wood for the fireplaces was an ongoing chore. The cable system was invaluable because nearly all the wood came from the mesa.

People have lived in here perhaps two hundred, well since 1200 . . . and when we came here there was almost no wood.

Wood was brought to the canyon rim, cut into usable lengths with a gasoline-powered saw, then loaded into the cable box and lowered into the canyon. The pickup truck took it to the lodge and cabins.

3. At Home in Frijoles Canyon

When George and Evelyn Frey came into Frijoles Canyon in May 1925, their son Richard (often called Dick or Dickie) was ten months old. Basic responsibility for his care fell to Evelyn. He was a bright, inquisitive child who was the center of his mother's life. One early incident when he was two or three years old stuck in Evelyn's memory.

I remember one time getting up to look at my baby—and he wasn't in the crib, and we were having a hard rain. It frightened me to death. And I could track him down the canyon just a little way from the home. . . . I looked and looked and kept on tracking him a little bit, and I came over and he was standing watching this thing [the stream] overflow. It must have been five or six feet deep. He had a little nightgown on, standing there watching the water.

As Richard got older he roamed among the caves, played in the river, and climbed the cliffs—typical kid activities. He had his own farm chores; this was a working ranch and everyone did his share. His closest companions were probably the ranch animals—dogs, cats, cows, horses. Sometimes he would explore and share his discoveries with the children arriving as visitors.

My little son found those arrow shafts; it was a little tight place in the rock, a kind of opening that didn't come clear together, and he came in one morning with these arrows.They'd been up there all this time and nobody had ever found them. He was over with a little boy playing.

The canyon summers were carefree. His mother later related one of his activities.

He and the chef built up a little dam of rocks and the water wasn't very deep, but we had an old telephone that had gone out, one of those kind that you wind when you want to talk to somebody. He had a negative wire on one side of the river and a positive on the

*other. He had a little bucket, so he would wind this thing and little
fish would come clear out of the water. They had four or five little
fish. He said, 'Mother, don't you understand this?'*

Because of the isolation of Frijoles Canyon it was not possible for
Richard to attend public school, and the Los Alamos Ranch School
was very expensive. Evelyn responded to an advertisement in the
New York Times for the Calvert (correspondence) School out of
Baltimore. She obtained certification in the Calvert system and home-
schooled Richard until he completed the fourth grade. She would
summon him with a bell to the little desk he used for his schoolwork.

*I did fairly well at school teaching, but it about killed me. . . . [I]
taught my child through the fourth grade and he was two grades
ahead.*

The Calvert system for kindergarten through eighth grade must
have been northern New Mexico's home school of choice. The Pack
family, who ran Ghost Ranch at Abiquiu, also taught their children
using this system. The Calvert School is still in business today.

The Freys provided their own social life and entertainment. At the
end of a full day, a good dinner and conversation were often adequate
rewards for hard work. Reading was a cherished pastime. After
dark they read by lantern light because there was no electricity.

*We had these Coleman lights and they are just wonderful lights to
read by. You have to pump them up all the time and about the
time you get one fixed, that little mantle falls off and you go to
work again and fix it up, and we had a dozen of them all over the
place.*

The lodge housed a small library of books brought in by the
Freys or left by guests. The family also subscribed to the *New York
Times* and the *Albuquerque Journal*.

One time we had a man come in at the old place, and there was a table with the New York Times *on it and he kept looking at it and he said he just wanted to know a little more about it. And I said, 'Well, son, I'm going to tell you something. I take it.'*

This was Meyer Berger, a reporter who later became a Pulitzer Prize winner and editor of the *New York Times*. He asked Evelyn to write her story for the paper. He said he would see that it got printed; he would even get her an editor. Berger suggested in a letter to her that it would bring "a neat little income." Evelyn never did write her story, but the paper ran a full page ad entitled, "She climbs out of a canyon to get the *New York Times*," and illustrated it with a drawing of a woman walking out of a canyon. (See Illustration14.)

Every three weeks (six in the winter), George picked up the mail. The news was always late. Not that it mattered; any news was welcome whenever it came. George and Evelyn and the help would put a sizable log in the fireplace and sit and read by the Coleman lanterns.

Everybody had their lamp and everybody sat around, and if we had guests, we did the same thing. Because there's nothing to do and we had no TV at that time, of course.

The Freys did not bring a radio with them in 1925. They had a gramophone, a windup record player, but no means of outside entertainment. One old gentleman and his son from Hot Springs, Arkansas, sought to remedy the deficit.

He just couldn't imagine anyone living without one [a radio]. When he got ready to leave he presented me with this little radio. We had an old broken down cot beside the fireplace and Mr. Frey did something, hooked it into a wire [antenna] or something. . . . But I recall when he gave it to me I thought, 'Well, what can I give you in return?' And I had quite a nice pot by Maria of San Ildefonso. I gave it to him. I gave him a pot that would be worth $5,000 now.

George's antenna consisted of a wire crossing the canyon above the lodge connected to another wire coming down into the house to the crystal-set radio.

I still see the piece of iron sticking up in the rock. . . . Well, he shot a— I don't know how he did it—a wire across the canyon and also anchored it on, way up, and our antenna went right straight up one hundred feet.

One night Evelyn, nursing a toothache, was lying by the fireplace listening to the radio.

And I was listening to this—there had been some little article stating they would like to have letters from different parts of the world suggesting the music that Admiral Byrd should hear in the Antarctic or Arctic, wherever he was. I had very fancy stationery [designed by a friend] and I sent in my suggestions. I'm sure it was my stationery and certainly not what I told him, but I got the prize.

During the summer months, especially, the Freys could be entertained by their guests. Often after an evening meal, guests would delight both canyon residents and themselves by telling stories and swapping experiences. Visitors came from many part s of the world. The variety, courtesy and sophistication they brought with them brightened the routine of everyday life in the canyon.

Casual visiting back and forth with local neighbors rarely occurred. There were no close neighbors and a visit meant a journey up and down the trail and a ride over dusty roads. Local folks, however, were attracted to the Sunday noon meals served at the Frijoles Canyon Lodge. The Freys, for their part, enjoyed the Sunday evening dinners served at the Los Alamos Ranch School.

We, as a family, would go occasionally; . . . it was always served outside, and my, what meals!

The ranch school boys often came to Frijoles Canyon for Friday evening dinner and stayed through lunch Sunday.

And we were all just half dead when they left for taking care of them.

Peggy Pond Church and her children from the Los Alamos Ranch School visited occasionally. So, too, did the Francis Smithwicks, who lived on the north mesa top in the "old Loomis place" (Anchor Ranch). Mr. Smithwick was a major in the English army; his wife was a nurse. The Smithwicks entertained a lot, inviting local people to dinners and parties.

Edith Warner, another neighbor, lived at Otowi Crossing. Warner had a small tea room which became locally famous during World War II as a place for Manhattan Project scientists to relax and enjoy dinner. Peggy Pond Church immortalized Warner in her book, *The House at Otowi Bridge.*[5] Evelyn often stopped in at the tea room on her return trips from Santa Fe.

The last time I went to see her, she was dying of cancer and her sister asked me if I minded not going—she had become frail. She did much good for everyone that came into her life, including [sharing] her chocolate cake [recipe]. And I tried it out a time or two and it went flat on me.[6]

Telephone communication in these years was primitive. There were actually three rudimentary systems and three phones going in and out of Frijoles Canyon.

One [system] went directly from our place here into Lamy and then into Santa Fe. You'd just ring the thing and Santa Fe would say, 'Number?' I liked that.

The Santa Fe line traveled east along the mesa north of Frijoles Canyon to the Rio Grande, hanging from trees and limbs and anything else that would hold it above ground. It extended across the river and up the far mesa to the Pankey property on the top, where it could continue on to Lamy.

I don't know whether anybody would ever remember him [Mr. Pankey] or not, but he had, I believe, the largest fenced pasture in the United States,one hundred and eighty thousand acres. And I remember that instead of having gates for automobiles, there were troughs—I think that's what you'd call them. You had to hit those troughs [cattle guards] to go over. He lived across the Rio Grande.[7]

A second telephone line went to the Jemez Mountain back country. This was a real party line. Different rings identified who was being called.

My number was very interesting due to the fact that somebody was calling to tell me that they would come to the lodge. Everybody listened. . . . You could hear babies crying, roosters crowing, people talking, but we were all used to that and everybody did it, don't you see?

Once, a young couple who had just been engaged became separated. The woman was in Santa Fe; the man was ill in the Jemez backcountry.

But our telephone into Santa Fe and the one into the Jemez [were] right close together and I could just talk to either one of them. I carried on a very flourishing romance. . . . So I talked to her and I gave him kisses and love, very beautiful. . . . And I never met either of them. But I carried this on all winter. It turned out very well. . . . One time they came to the top of the canyon and called down (this was the telephone from the top down) telling me there was a package of mine. It was a beautiful box of candy there. But they lived like this. I knew them after awhile.

Keeping the outside phone lines working was a constant battle.

And the people that would come out getting wood from [the] . . . little settlements, if their wagon broke down, they would just reach up and cut a bunch of telephone wire . . . and fix their wagon. So Mr. Frey was forever having to swim across the Rio Grande on a horse [to fix the line].

The third telephone line was unique to Frijoles Canyon. George ran a cable from the top of the canyon rim down to the lodge lobby.

*When a group would come in they would call down and tell us how
many there were for lunch, because they sure had to eat lunch at
our house. . . . They would ring at the top of the cliff . . . down to our
old lodge, and we'd send . . . horses up to bring down the guests
that couldn't walk in or out.*

Although summer was the busiest time in Frijoles Canyon, the winter
off-season was challenging in a different way. It was cold and darkness
came early—especially in the canyon bottom, where the sun descended
behind the cliffs by midafternoon.

*The sun goes out of here—well, a little before three o'clock in
the afternoon, and you put on your lights and turn up the heat and
get ready for a very long evening.*

Evelyn kept a few of her chickens over the winter, probably for eggs.
Cattle and pigs provided staple meats in the colder winter months. The
Frey cattle foraged on the mesa south of the canyon.

*The Indians had cows up there, too. They didn't run away. . . . In the
wintertime sometimes, we would feed [them]. We'd send up hay. I
know Mr. Frey would say, once in a while, 'Well, so-and-so had a
calf and it's about six months old, but she doesn't have it now.'*

George butchered and dressed a beef in late fall and hung it in a
small screen-enclosed building. A roast or steak was sawed off the
frozen carcass as needed. Deer hunting provided venison to supplement
the beef.
    Wild Merriam turkeys were abundant in the canyon. Prehistoric
Indians had made holding pens for them, keeping them possibly for food
but certainly for their feathers, which were used in ceremonies and in
blanket making. The Freys were very aware of these birds and even fed
them at times. They might even snag a wild turkey for Thanksgiving.

I recall one time we, at Thanksgiving, had no turkey and the snow was about, oh, four or five inches deep. So I said to Mr. Frey, 'I hear the turkeys crossing the canyon.' They would go across for feed. He went to the kitchen door and shot a great big fat gobbler, and I told him, 'Talk about the pilgrims!'

4. The Park Service Comes

The years 1925 to 1931 must have been magical in Frijoles Canyon. The Freys were masters of their own destiny. Work and problems were theirs alone to solve in this special place. But the year 1932 would bring changes. Evelyn Frey would be thrust for the rest of her life into the public eye. Except for her family and a very few close friends, she chose to be "Mrs. Frey" even to those who knew her well in daily life. A warm, generous woman, nonetheless she had an old-fashioned reserve.

On February 25, 1932, President Herbert Hoover, by Executive Proclamation, removed Bandelier National Monument from the Santa Fe National Forest and put it under the direction of the National Park Service. Frank Pinkley managed the fourteen National Park Service areas in the southwest. Known as a tenacious, blunt perfectionist, he envisioned that Bandelier would become the entry point for visitors coming to southwest areas. For this to happen, development of visitor-use facilities was absolutely necessary.

When the Park Service took over Bandelier, the existing facilities, except for the Forest Service ranger station, belonged to the concessionaires, George and Evelyn Frey. The buildings were adequate but somewhat ramshackle. To Pinkley, the canyon floor—with cattle, chickens, orchard, garden, corrals, and sheds—resembled a homestead. Pinkley also felt that the lodge area was too close to Tyuonyi, the large prehistoric community house.

Park Service rangers, like the Forest Service rangers before them, did not initially live in the park all year. A ranger generally arrived around the first of May and left sometime after Labor Day. Some were married; some even had families. The superintendent listed ranger wives as Honorary Custodians Without Pay (HCWP). It must have been a welcome change for Evelyn Frey and her housekeeper to have other women in the canyon.

Ed Rogers was one of the first Park Service summer rangers. He reported his arrival:

The wind was blowing so hard that Mr. Frey was afraid to operate

29

the cable by which our belongings are brought into the canyon. We had to wait until sundown for the wind to die down. Instead of getting settled by night we moved in after dark.[8]

Ed and his new wife Gay lived in the old Forest Service cabin up-canyon from the lodge. Ranger duties were varied and included erecting signs, repairing ladders, checking bridges, and cleaning brush out of Tyuonyi. As in Forest Service days, the ranger's main duty was greeting visitors at the bottom of the trail.

He sat here and watched people come down the trail. Then he stopped them and then he told them, 'The trail is up there farther now.' What to do, don't you see? Then he'd come back down and set himself down again, and that was his work all day.

The six hundred thirty-four visitors in September 1933 marked a sixteen percent increase over the number of visitors in September 1932. Word came to the Freys that there would be a winter Civilian Conservation Corps (CCC) camp at Bandelier with about two hundred men. According to his monthly report, Rogers hoped this additional help would mean that sixty to eighty miles of trails could be rebuilt and debris on the canyon floor cleaned up.

But on October 16, 1933, Ed Rogers, for unknown reasons, unexpectedly committed suicide. Gay Rogers ran frantically to the lodge.

'Oh', she said, 'Mrs. Frey, my husband has killed himself.' I said, 'Gay, what are you saying? What is going on?' And I could hardly walk, but, anyhow, I went out to the laundry building on a little hill and they could see me from the top of the cable. . . . There were four or five men up there letting down lumber. I began to yell, 'Help, help,' and throw my hands up. . . . Mr. Frey turned off the engine and these men came right down the hill, right down the side of the cliff. And I got her up there, but before I got to this house, I could hear him moaning. So I put her in the kitchen and I told her to stay there, and I went into the bedroom. And he was lying—he was in uniform, stretched out. His hands were down. . . . Half of his head

was on the wall, and a pistol [was] over there. I stayed with him until he died. And then Mr. Frey strapped him on a board and then took him out with a cable. They were young people.[9]

The CCC provided Pinkley and the Park Service with funding and a work force. In October and November 1933, the army moved in with thirty men to construct temporary CCC camp buildings and build latrines. The crews lived in the lodge, moving into their new buildings as they became available.

Another camp was being constructed above the CCC camp for the Civil Works Authority (CWA), forerunner of the Works Progress Administration (WPA). The Southwest Monument Monthly Report for January 1934 reported on these activities.

[Workers] cleared out Mr. Frey's stable, boarded up some sheds, and made bunks out of odds and ends of lumber. There [are] bunks for 64 men by staggering work periods. The entire force is eating at Frey's hotel for $0.25 per meal per person.[10]

The Freys raised the meal rate from seventy-five cents a day to a dollar a day after the government pulled out the CWA workers who had been helping with kitchen duties. The CCC promptly objected to the price increase, and the Freys agreed to return to the seventy-five cents a day. Mrs. Frey refunded the difference.

As CCC crew accommodations were completed, the men began other projects. These included eradicating tent caterpillars, working on the phone line, removing barns and other buildings in the canyon, and stabilizing the ruins. Drinking water was still drawn from the Rito de los Frijoles, but the CCC built underground storage tanks to eliminate freezing. Other projects were also started during this period; projects under way when funding was requested were usually automatically approved.

"Boss" Pinkley wanted all visitors, including those who were less active, infirm, or older, to have access to the canyon floor. An entrance road was central to his plans. He saw the road as the key to increasing the number of visitors, a number which he envisioned might even exceed fifteen thousand a year! His plan succeeded beyond his wildest dreams. During the mid to late 1990s, the number of people visiting Bandelier averaged three hundred eighty thousand per year.

Probably the most essential project, both for Pinkley's plans and for the crews' work, was providing automotive access to the canyon. Park Service staff and George Frey reviewed several possible routes into the park. They chose the present eastern route because it gave the best view of the canyon on rounding the northern rim, it would not interfere with planned buildings, and it was the least intrusive on the landscape.

On December 9, 1933, a narrow twelve-foot-wide truck trail became passable. The CCC staff convinced Mrs. Frey that she needed to go to Santa Fe for supplies that morning. When she returned, she was diverted to the new road.

> On the 9th the first car drove down into the canyon. This honor was reserved for engineer [Walter] Attwell and he had with him Mrs. Frey, who operates the hotel known as the Frijoles Canyon Ranch. She said she had been waiting 9 years for this.[11]

> *I know I came over it before it was paved. . . . It was decided that I should be the first one to come down this road here, and I think there were chuckholes this deep. I began to think we weren't going to make it in that little space, but we did.*

A few months later the truck trail was widened to twenty-two feet. As soon as the road into the canyon opened, the number of visitors rose. In March 1934, there were two hundred eighty visitors. The number rose month by month, reaching two thousand one hundred twenty-five in August. During postseason October 1934, eight hundred three people arrived, compared with three hundred forty in October 1933. Many of the visitors came in Harvey Detour groups, which now arrived almost daily.

The road also made daytime use more feasible. People could come into the canyon for a picnic or lunch at the lodge and be back at their homes that night. Bandelier was being used as a city park.

Initial plans for the area intended that the Freys' lodge operation would remain where it was, across the stream from the Tyuonyi ruins. But Pinkley believed that the best way for visitors to achieve an understanding of the canyon's prehistoric inhabitants was for the Park Service to provide the only access to the ruins. If an auto trail went directly to the Frey lodge through the proposed campground, visitors could easily by-pass Park Service contact. Very soon a new Frijoles Canyon Lodge and a new parking lot appeared in the plans for the administrative compound.

The Freys were subject to Park Service jurisdiction. Conversely, the Park Service was bound by the Freys' 1925 ninety-nine-year Forest Service lease and had to replace any facilities it destroyed. Ranger Jared Morse reported one negotiation in the summer of 1934.

> During his visit here, Mr. Pinkley, Mr. Attwell and I arranged with Mr. Frey to clear up the present Hotel utility area. In return for their existing buildings we will build one building containing a stable, hay lift, saddle and feed room, small chicken coop, caretaker's room and corral. The building will be on an approved location up canyon between the hotel and the ranger cabin.[12]

The proposed stable was subsequently relocated down canyon from the other buildings.

Activity in Frijoles Canyon during this time occurred on two levels. On one level, the CCC and CWA continued work on the road and began constructing the compound buildings, starting with the administration/museum building. On the other, they also began work on a campground and comfort station. The campsites had cement picnic tables and fireplaces, and the comfort station included showers and laundry facilities. Today the campground is the picnic area and the comfort station is the picnic area restroom.

The old Frijoles Canyon Lodge still operated, hosting overnight guests and many more day visitors, but it had an added dimension. The CCC camp at Frijoles contained from two hundred to three hundred boys at any given time, young men in their late teens and early twenties. They received room and board and were paid $1.00 per day; $25.00 of their earnings were automatically sent monthly to their families. Most were local men living in communities up and down the Rio Grande. Most did not have transportation of their own, so they often stayed in the canyon during weekends.

We had our large portal and during the CCC period here, there were, at one time, three hundred fifty of our young men, and a good many were out of little towns that were near. And those were very hard times for almost everyone. And this large portal of ours, those who lived nearby, the army would take them home during the weekend, but those who couldn't go home sat on my portal. And I've looked out there many times during the weekend; they were sitting just as thickly as they could sit on this portal. And we had a graphanola that you could do this-a-way [wind-up], and to this day I can still hear 'The Man on the Flying Trapeze.' I thought I was going to lose my mind, but they had no place to go and we always welcomed them, and they were fine young men.

The buildings in the canyon were constructed in a style termed pueblo revival. Even though the bricks look like adobe, they are really tuff, compacted volcanic ash, quarried on the mesa top just outside the northern park boundary.

It is tufa [tuff], so you can saw them and they work easily, too. They used to put them in tubs of water, don't quite know why. Maybe they would work easier. They would use big saws.

Later, after the park was enlarged, Juniper campground was built in the quarry area. The quarry itself is now the monument amphitheater.

After a full day's work, the CCC boys needed entertainment and diversion. According to the monument's May 1934 monthly report,

An old field, near the camp, was converted into a baseball diamond and several teams organized. Two tennis courts were built on the camp grounds—one clay and one asphalt. Several horseshoe courts are in process.[13]

In June 1934 the CCC made a swimming pool by constructing a concrete dam on the Rito de los Frijoles about one-half mile below the camp.

We did have a nice swimming pool. It must have been about ten foot deep, and I used to go fishing and all I had to do was to sit down and catch my limit of fish right while I sat still.

With some changes, the Freys continued on in the canyon. George's cable system departed with the coming of the road. There is no mention of it again in the records. Before its departure, however, the cable had helped haul out not only Ed Rogers' body, but a Park Service ranger who had been hurt.

This Park Service man by the name of Tom Vint climbed up a pinon tree, why I didn't know, and he fell out and was not seriously injured, but he didn't feel very well. . . . In putting Tom in the basket we had no place for his head, so I put his hat in and pushed it down and put his head right there.

The old utility area on the north mesa top, which included storage sheds at the top of the cable, was removed and the push to "tidy up" the Frey areas progressed. The lodge continued operating and likely had more guests than before. There were certainly more lunch guests because of road access. The garden still had to be tended, the orchard maintained, and the livestock fed. The CCC had already brought in electricity, so daily life was somewhat easier.

In 1934 Richard was ten years old. He had completed fourth grade under his mother's tutelage. That year, with the new road open, he began school in Santa Fe.

I boarded him with a family in Santa Fe. . . . He was a wonderful student and I had him ready to go into public school. And then if the snow wasn't too deep I just went and got my son on Friday night and took him back Monday morning into Santa Fe.

Richard stayed in the canyon during the summer. A park superintendent related a typical summer incident.

A lady walking along the cliffs asked if the Indians were having a pow-wow or a dance across the canyon. She asked what the whoops and cries were. It happened to be Mrs. Frey's little boy, home on summer vacation.[14]

After 1935 the records no longer mention George Frey. Mrs. Frey always referred only obliquely to his departure.

And that has made a very interesting life here. But it's had its tragedies too. Mr. Frey went away in '35.

There is no way to know the exact reason for George's leaving, but by piecing together fragments we can create a possible scenario. It was Evelyn Frey's decision to come into the canyon. George was not a farm person, but he quickly saw where he could be useful—designing and installing the cable, telephone, and irrigation systems; making repairs; caring for the stock; hunting. His mechanical abilities were critical. When the Park Service entered the picture after 1932, he may have felt that his expertise was not needed. His morale must have been affected by having his cable system dismantled and the outbuildings "cleaned up." He tried to work for the CCC for a short period, but didn't continue.

We know nothing of George and Evelyn Frey's personal life as a couple. Perhaps this was coming, and when George could see that his wife and child would not be alone in the canyon, he felt he could leave. Mrs. Frey always said that he was a city man and she was a country woman. Whatever the reasons for leaving, leave he did—evidently not to step back into the Frijoles Canyon picture. Possibly out of a continuing concern for Richard and his mother, George left behind a valuable deer rifle. The rifle was one of several intended by the Remington Arms Company for the last czar of Russia. After the czar's execution, the rifles were sold to the National Rifle Association, which sold them to their members.

The lodge guest register (Appendix A) records some of the people who visited during all the construction activity in Frijoles. The Southwest Monuments Monthly Report also lists Park Service people of note who visited Bandelier. Some were regular visitors: Walter Attwell, engineer for the road; Frank Pinkley, Superintendent of Southwest Monuments; Chuck Richey, landscaper for the Park Service; and CCC officials on monthly camp inspections.

In mid-1935 Mrs. Frey agreed to move her operations to a new lodge that would be closer to the main parking plaza. She thought that business would improve and that she and the Park Service could cooperate better. In November 1935, the Park Service and Mrs. Frey agreed on a proposal for a twenty-year lease to operate the new lodge. The concession fee would be $10 a year.

On May 16, 1939, Mrs. Frey formally took possession of the concessions and the new lodge. According to the monuments monthly report,

> Eight cabins are ready for occupancy and meals are served at both the lunch counter and dining room. A good collection of Indian rugs and jewelry are on display in the sales room. This new lodge is quite the modern thing with an exterior appearance of very old Mexican and Indian architecture. All visitors exclaim at the grand workman-ship done by Superintendent [H. B.] Chase, his technical foreman, and CCC enrollees. We all hope and are quite certain that Mrs. Frey will make a success of her large undertaking.[15]

On May 29, 1939, Evelyn Frey moved to the new lodge, leaving a home and life that she had loved.

> Immediately following [her move] work was started demolishing the old hotel area and today all buildings are completely demolished, the salvaged materials stacked and a large amount of the debris hauled from the canyon.[16]

> *I didn't want the old house torn away. It was still a very lovely*

house. But they tore it all down in one day and I said, 'Well, why so hurried?' And they said, 'Well, Mrs. Frey, you'd go home if we didn't tear it down'. And I would have, too. I did like that place so very much. . . . My [old] place here; I just pled with him, a certain man, to leave that. . . . I just pled for that building. Now the Park Service wouldn't touch it because it was built in 1908.

Landscaping followed close upon demolition.

Three crews of approximately 10 men each have been used in landscaping three areas—Mrs. Frey's garden, the recently completed stables and the residential area. The garden was heavily planted in an effort to screen it. The road to this area was blocked by planting trees.[17]

Destruction of the old lodge remained a poignant, vivid memory in Mrs. Frey's life, one she carried with her always. She probably never totally forgave Frank Pinkley, "a certain man," even though she could see that the action was inevitable.

5. Prelude to World War II

By 1940 the canyon held sixteen new buildings. For Mrs. Frey they included eight guest cabins, a hotel lobby and curio shop, a dining room and kitchen, and her new quarters.

A museum building was completed after several changes in the design. The CCC enclosed the space between the administration building and the museum, planned originally as a drive-through to the campground. When the museum was ready for exhibits, the Park Service hired Pablita Velarde to paint illustrations for the cases. Velarde, a young woman from Santa Clara Indian Pueblo, later become a well-known New Mexico artist. This was her first commission, one she would work at off and on for several years. These early illustrations are considered among her finest work.

The CCC not only built the park's structural complex, but they also crafted the tin light fixtures, curtain rods, and wood decorations in the cabins, lobby, and dining room. The furniture was also made within the park. The cabins had wooden beds, dressers, chairs, wood boxes, and desks—all carved and painted or stained. Mrs. Frey purchased wood and had the CCC boys make furniture for her apartment in the same style.

Under the CCC the young men were learning lifelong skills.

[At the beginning] they had no more idea how to make a stone floor or a ceiling with vigas and finish their walls. They had no trade, and most of them were natives, Spanish Americans. But when they went away they could make their own livelihood making furniture. I recall the man that was overseeing it. It had to be just so or it just went right back again and they worked it over again. And then they had a tin project here. The chandeliers in this room look like Mexico, but they weren't. They were made here.

Even though the Park Service built a new lodge to replace the old one, it appears that Mrs. Frey received payment for the old lodge. A torn

39

sheet of paper in the archives at Bandelier has the figure $19,766.59 written on it. Down the side, in Evelyn Frey's handwriting, is this note:

Total paid me for my old ranch—O me how I lost but there was no one to ever help me.[18]

The final action necessary to remove evidence of the twentieth century from the area around Tyuonyi was to eliminate Mrs. Frey's orchard.

Then when the Park Service took over, the gentleman who was in here that was doing this negotiation with me, he was going to cut the trees down, and I said, 'You just give me time to pack a suitcase, because I'm going to go out, too,' and he left the trees. But they took the water off. Many of the tender trees died, but the apple trees are persistent and they're covered with apples this year.

There is no listing of what was moved from the old lodge to the new, but quantity and quality were much different in the new lodge. In the new lodge Mrs. Frey could feed one hundred fifty people and house eighty guests.

Probably one of her first decisions dealt with dishes for the dining room. She used the turkey design that she had earlier employed for her curtains, a turkey with a broken circle around it.

I used this design here, make a circle like the Indian—they leave an opening in the circle and if tragedy or unhappiness happens it has a way out. Also if happiness has come to you it has a way in. Might as well think that way instead of thinking, I'm going to have it forever. . . . I wish I had kept the correspondence when I had my dishes made. Whoever was going to work on the design, he wanted to know what was wrong with the circle. I would write back and tell him. Then I would get a shipment and the circle would be closed. Then I'd fuss again, don't you see? But the dishes were very pretty.

In the old lodge, Mrs. Frey had sewn the curtains herself, but for the new lodge she had curtains made in Albuquerque. She ordered linens

40

from Denver. The rooms were furnished with the handmade furniture made by the CCC and decorated with Navajo rugs and paintings by Caroline Pickard of Santa Fe.

A commercial laundry washed the lodge linens. Mrs. Frey found the arrangement a source of both amusement and consternation.

> *They had their own linen, and I was the only one who owned my linen, so I was just a bedevilment to them. But as long as I operated, they came and got my linen and took care of me. I recall one time I said to [my helper]Geronima, 'I hope we get our new sheets back,' but I don't think we got many of them back. I'd get sheets from Socorro and different hospitals and all this business, but we got by anyhow.*

The lodge remained open all winter that first year. According to the monument's monthly report for November 1939,

> Although travel is not as heavy as during the summer months, a higher percentage of tourists are taking advantage of the accommodations than did during the summer months.[19]

At the end of construction the CCC moved their camp buildings to Water Canyon, nine and one-half miles by road from Frijoles Canyon. With the completion of the moving, razing, and re-vegetation of the CCC camp site, Frijoles Canyon was ready to take on its new Park Service look, that of a pueblo revival "village."

An abundance of wild animals lived in the canyon when Mrs. Frey was at the old lodge. These disappeared with the construction activity in the canyon. When the CCC barracks were moved out, the animals began to come back. The monthly report for January 1940 noted,

> A flock of twenty wild Merriam turkeys took up residence in the developed area. So well do the hotel and buildings fit in with the 'natural' that the turkeys were right at home on the hotel, flying from building to building and running through the patios.[20]

Local Indians still brought their goods to Mrs. Frey at her gift shop in the new lodge. She would buy items and put them in her basement until she had room in the shop.

They'll have a square of calico and put their pottery in it and carry it in that manner. They bring down pottery and blankets and this and that. . . . I always felt so bad if I didn't buy something. . . . I had a brother [Hugh] that bought lots of things for me and he had a fine understanding of Indian arts and crafts. I had a nice collection of Hopi woven baskets. I had labor baskets that I sold for $25.00; now they'd sell for $2,000.00. At that time our artifacts were within reason. I had one of the loveliest gift shops in all this country. Just beautiful.

It appears that there was a difference in what the guests expected between the old and the new lodge. At the old lodge, isolation and seclusion were the goals; at the new, the atmosphere was more that of a hotel, with guests expecting occasional entertainment. Several people from the different Indian pueblos worked for Mrs. Frey. They would bring their costumes and entertain the guests with traditional dancing.

There were a couple of Indians [Pat and Romolo Cordero] that danced beautifully and one [Pat] sang. He made a recording, but I don't know what went with his recordings. . . .The two were working here, and they'd have dances in the evening once in a while. And occasionally at the noon hour, maybe we'd have a special party out and they'd dance awhile in the farthest patio. . . . I recall one time we had a Japanese party in here. One was an opera singer, and the chef happened to be someplace around over here looking around. He said he thought somebody was dying. But [it was] the singer—he was singing out here. . . . Occasionally of an evening we would have an entertainment and make a fire here and we had chairs and benches out here. And people always loved the evenings that we entertained here.

In addition to asking some of the canyon workers from the pueblos to perform for visitors, Mrs. Frey arranged for other dancers from the nearby villages to perform on weekends. A pueblo family arriving for the weekend would stay with her in her apartment. Usually children did some of the dancing, and Mrs. Frey would give them little baskets to hold money collected from the audience. In most instances, the parents used this money to purchase necessities like shoes and clothes for their children.

Running the new lodge was different from running the old. For one thing, more helpers had to be fed, housed, and managed. Mrs. Frey had hired an Indian couple, Emiliano and Geronima, from San Juan Indian Pueblo to help her with housekeeping and maintenance. They were with her for a number of years, living in the canyon.

> *Geronima and her husband, Emiliano, kept our rooms. They were beautifully clean and our linen was always nicer—and they lived right here with me, don't you see? They had their own apartment. . . . Eighteen years, she told me, she and her husband kept house for me. We had twenty rooms and six of them, I believe, could take six people in each one if I bedded them proper, the big ones. But they were wonderful help and very dependable people. She's the only one that I had that would ever mend linen. After she left, I don't think I ever had a piece of linen mended after that. But she just watched her linen like it was hers and it was always [neat]. I had a little electric [sewing] machine; she just loved that little machine. She was scared to death of the thing for a while, until my sister-in-law taught her to not be afraid of it and work with it.*

The old Frijoles Canyon Lodge operated year round. With the Freys living in the building, there was no reason to close it, whether customers were there or not. The situation was different after the new lodge was built. Without a fair number of guests, the lodge could not profitably stay open. The monument's monthly reports for October and November 1940 announced,

> For the first time in many years, the lodge will close for the winter. Closing date is announced for Nov. 1 and the lodge probably will reopen May 1, 1941 on a restricted basis. Full operation will not commence until June first.[21]
>
> Frijoles Canyon Lodge closed Nov. 1st and Mrs. Frey is taking a much needed vacation in Denver.[22]

The year 1940 ended with the world in turmoil, but with Bandelier National Monument ready and poised to meet the next season. Its physical plant was nearly complete, visitors were coming, and it merited its first year-round ranger in November.

For Mrs. Frey, 1940 marked a more personal change. In early September Richard left for school at the New Mexico Military Institute in Roswell, southern New Mexico.

There came a time when he was about fifteen and I had to place
him someplace where someone would take care of him, but he didn't
like that military.

By 1941 the old CCC camp was no longer part of the canyon. The camp already had been moved onto Forest Service land, and the plan was for it to be turned over to the Forest Service in June 1940. That deadline was extended to enable the CCC to build the Bandelier fire tower and custodian's residence. During the spring of 1941 the monument closed down while the CCC fought floods in Española, hauled wood into Frijoles Canyon to keep rooms warm enough to dry paint, finished residences, and worked on the sewage disposal system and miscellaneous projects. The monument's own work force was custodial—repairing and maintaining monument buildings.

The CCC camp in Water Canyon was terminated June 26, 1941, and camp buildings turned over to the Forest Service. When the United States entered World War II, the CCC itself was disbanded. The young men generally joined the armed services. Equipment and supplies were transferred to the war effort. It is worth noting that the grand scale of work by the CCC at Bandelier National Monument was never to be repeated anywhere else in the National Park System.

Travel into Bandelier during 1941 after the late opening was much less than during previous years. The depressed economic state of the United States was now combined with the uncertain threat of world war. Moreover, road conditions between the canyon and Santa Fe were worse than usual because of a severe winter and spring. Paving did not extend much beyond Pojoaque, and washouts and high centers were prevalent the rest of the way.

Mrs. Frey considered raising rates for the 1941 season because of increased costs and fewer visitors. A sampling of the rates is shown from her January 24, 1941, proposal to the Park Service.[23]

Rooms

Room without bath	1 double bed, 1 person	$ 1.75/day
	3 persons, extra bed	2.50/day
Room with private bath	1 double bed, 1 person	3.00/day
	3 persons, extra bed	4.00/day
Deluxe cabin	livingroom, bedroom, twin beds, private bath	10.00/day

Meals

Breakfast	$ 0.75
Lunch	1.00
Dinner	1.25

Sandwiches

Hamburger	0.10
Hot roast beef w/mashed potatoes & gravy	0.30

Coffee	0.05
Bottled soft drinks	0.10

The lodge closed for the winter in the late fall of 1941. The monument custodian also closed the visitor center until the following March. This held down costs (heeding a federal nondefense activities directive) while still allowing the monument crew to perform needed maintenance. Following the entry of the United States into World War II on December 7, 1941, the park staff gathered scrap iron, rubber, copper, and brass for the war effort. They planted a victory garden in Mrs. Frey's old orchard, but even with an eight-foot-high fence, bears, deer, raccoons, and turkeys ate most of the produce.

In 1942 the lodge did open but to slow business. Bad weather, tire and gas shortages, and rationing limited the lodge to even fewer visitors than it had in 1941. It closed in September, earlier than usual. Despite these difficulties, Bandelier National Monument and Frijoles Canyon Lodge had not been drastically affected by the first year of the war.

6. World War II and Los Alamos

In a letter to his mother dated April 2, 1942, Richard talked about coming home for vacation, his desire to be a major in the army, and what he intended to do when he got to the front lines. He said that he had his dad's address in Hermosa, California, and had received several letters from him. He closed his letter with, "Just you remember that I will always be with you even if something does happen to me in war; not even death can separate us."[24] It seems quite clear that Richard intended to go into the armed services.

In December 1942 the army took over the nearby Los Alamos Ranch School for a secret project involving the war effort. In early 1943 it began to quietly move in equipment and scientists. Bandelier's acting custodian, Chester A. (Art) Thomas, offered the army assistance but felt that his offer was not welcome. The relationship improved only after the new Los Alamos personnel began informing Bandelier staff of any activity that might affect the park.

The number of people moving into Los Alamos far exceeded the available housing there. One attractive solution was to use Frijoles Canyon Lodge. On May 24, 1943, J. Robert Oppenheimer, director of the Los Alamos project, announced to monument personnel that his project was authorized to operate the lodge. He wanted it open for project use by June 15.

So far Mrs. Frey had yet to manage the new lodge for a typical, full season. Consequently she was not in the canyon for the summer season when Oppenheimer issued his deadline.

> Well I was going to New York City, and I went by Santa Fe and told them [the project people] that I had heard that they were thinking about taking over the lodge, and I wanted to know about it. Of course, everything was so secretive in those days and I think maybe our secret of the atomic bomb perhaps is the best secret we ever kept. 'On, no, nothing like that.' Of course they knew it—that they were going to do it, but they didn't tell me. So I flew to New

47

*York City and . . . I went into the hotel. I had a friend there—well,
she had lived in New York City most of her life—she had tickets for
some shows and that's one reason I went.*

*They handed me a note and I thought of Richard immediately,
and it was this thing to tell me to get on a plane. I think I had an
hour-and-a-half or two hours to get on a plane and come right
home, so that was my trip to New York City. So they put me on a
plane—I guess it was our plane [but] it was full of Canadian
officers; they had little red things up here on their collar. And I
looked like a little brown wren. I had a little brown hat setting up
there and I don't know what all. And I know that they wondered for
the life of them what I was doing on that [airplane] and I wondered
too—but anyhow, when I got to Albuquerque, there was a big car
there to meet me to dash me here. There was something—some
regulation that since I had the lease, they couldn't undo all my
doors and go in without my being there, don't you see?*

Mrs. Frey quickly inventoried everything in the lodge—dishes,
sheets, kitchen equipment, furniture. On June 3 she signed over the "right-
of-entry" to the army.

Oppenheimer asked Dorothy McKibbin, the popular receptionist
for the Los Alamos project office in Santa Fe since March 1943, to live in
Bandelier with her son Kevin during the summer. She was needed as a
buffer between the army and Mrs. Frey, who was disturbed by this large
group of people moving in.

Kevin McKibbin later became the chief ranger at Bandelier. Mrs.
Frey voiced her complaints over the disruption to him during a visit in
her old age.

*But they took everything over. They had no bedding. That's when
they broke all my beautiful dishes. They had nothing, and they
brought in the army. That's when your mother and I both worked
there for awhile. I couldn't do it, and I'm sure she didn't know a
kitchen either, but she worked there anyhow, and she was with the
people on top back there and it went pretty good. But when I'd
go in the kitchen, there'd be fifteen or twenty or forty or something
of soldiers in there, and I just decided I couldn't do that. I could*

manage my own kitchen, but I couldn't imagine working with them.
But it went rather nice.[25]

Mrs. Frey had to give up the gift shop.

I packed up the shop and put that away. . . . At that time we had
eighteen bunkbeds in there.

The project used other guest ranches in the area to house scientists
until facilities in Los Alamos could catch up with the needs, but Frijoles
Canyon Lodge was the closest and simplest to protect. The road and the
trail could easily be guarded against intruders. Regular visitors could enter
the park, but no food or lodging was available. These visitors often went
away furious, not only because of the lack of services but also because
the explanation was minimal.

The scientists' families much appreciated the cabins. Dr. Richard
Taschek, a nuclear physicist, and his family were typical. They stayed at
the lodge for several months from May to July 1943. The Tascheks had
a small baby, as did many of the others. There were no kitchen facilities in
the cabins and the mothers would gather in the kiva, the round building in
the middle of the housing compound, to warm milk on a hotplate. The
Tascheks had come from Princeton, where everything was rationed. They
were delighted to find that the army had no rationing and everyone had
meat at night. Meals were eaten in the dining room, after which the scientists
would gather to "talk shop." No outsiders were permitted. Parties and
dances, usually in the area off the dining room, provided entertainment.

Richard graduated from the New Mexico Military Institute in the
spring of 1943. He obtained employment at Los Alamos shortly after,
remaining until he entered the army in October 1943. In a remarkable
turn of events, he was also stationed at Los Alamos in the Special
Engineering Detachment (SED). The SED was created to augment the
scientific and technical personnel at Los Alamos with young men chosen
for their technical abilities. Many of its members went on to become
leading physicists, chemists, and metallurgists.

Mrs. Frey became personally acquainted with a number of project personnel, especially General Leslie R. Groves. General Groves had headed the team that built the Pentagon and now held overall responsibility for the work at Los Alamos.

And General Groves said, 'Now, everything is going to be all right, Mrs. Frey.' They had a little trouble with me because I didn't want to give up my place. But anyway, he'd come up to my room and just lie down on a big, old soft couch there. He was half dead all the time. I told him, 'You're just killing yourself right off here.' This was General Groves. He is gone now, too. 'Oh, no [replied Groves], you just wait 'till they get started in.' I said, 'Well what are you doing?' Of course, I knew he wasn't going to tell me what he was doing, because my son worked up there and I never knew one thing. It was a beautifully kept secret.

The McKee Construction Company housed Los Alamos workers in Bandelier during the winter of 1943-1944. In the spring of 1944 the army notified Mrs. Frey and the Park Service that it would need the lodge again that summer. However its use this time would not be so heavy, requiring only limited housing and provisions for breakfast and lunch. Although Mrs. Frey was upset about the situation, she worked better with the army in 1944.

And then they took it over a second time. That broke my heart. I had things strewn all over the place, and then they had to use it again because there was no bedding in Los Alamos and no place to eat either that would take care of the scientific world that we had there—and we had them all.

In mid-August of 1944 the army inventoried the lodge and moved out, retaining authority to use it for the 1945 season if needed. Because of that, the lodge did not open to the public the next spring and remained closed for the entire 1945 season.

The purpose of wartime Los Alamos was revealed in August. On August 6, 1945, the United States dropped an atom bomb on

Hiroshima; another was dropped three days later on Nagasaki. The war was over. Richard was now a sergeant at Los Alamos. For his mother, news of the Hiroshima and Nagasaki bombings explained Richard's wartime behavior.

I know [now] my young son also was working on the atomic, and he'd come in and change his clothes and then I knew he was ready— they were going to somewhere. I didn't know where. But he'd always say to me, 'Mother, I'll be back in a day or two.' But he witnessed, among the very few men in the army, the first explosion in White Sands.

A newspaper article in the *Santa Fe New Mexican* dated September 8, 1946, announced that four troop units at the "Los Alamos Atomic Bomb Laboratory" were given awards for "outstanding devotion to duty and maintenance of a high standard of discipline." Richard X. Frey from the Special Engineering Detachment was listed among these men.

With the war's end, Richard was transferred to Sandia base in Albuquerque, where he stayed until his discharge in April 1946. A picture of him at the time shows him in uniform and is labeled, "On furlough to California, 1945."

In January 1946 Mrs. Frey regained control of the lodge. The army allotted funds for repair and maintenance, but actual repairs were put off until the fall. Nonethless, there were a few visitors to both the park and the lodge.

A late summer picnic held in Frijoles Canyon included sixty-two of the nation's leading physicists. The event augmented a five-day conference in Los Alamos dealing with basic nuclear physics. Among those attending were Edward Teller, J. Robert Oppenheimer, and Robert R. Wilson. According to the August 1946 monthly report for the monument,

On August 21, 1946 we had a glittering array of scientists in the area. . . . There were 55 PhDs here at one time and 4 Nobel Prize winners including Dr. Ernest Lawrence and Dr. Fermi of atomic bomb fame.[26]

Years later a ghost of Mrs. Frey's contact with the galaxy of scientists at Los Alamos during World War II would surface in an uglier fashion. Mrs. Frey had become acquainted with Robert Oppenheimer before World War II, when a youthful Robert and his brother Frank would ride horses over to the Jemez area from their ranch in the Pecos Mountains. It could only have been a surprise to her when she received a phone call during the early 1950s saying that Robert Oppenheimer, director of one of the most sensitive war programs in the world's history, was being investigated as a spy. (He was later exonerated.) Many years afterwards, Mrs. Frey commented on the accusation.

> *I know there was a man called from California and he said, 'I want to know what you know about Mr. Oppenheimer.' and I said 'Well, sir, I'll just tell you right now, I don't know anything about him.' They came to see me and I said, 'Well, I'm telling you now, just as I told you before, with the scientists you did well if you got a nod out of them when you said good morning.*

To Mrs. Frey, intrusions such as this were unimportant blips in the flow of living. The watershed event of her life, one that would color all of her future days, occurred in 1947. Richard died unexpectedly.

The 1947 season at Bandelier began normally. The new lodge had not had a regular season with no outside pressures since its opening. By January 1947, Richard was working once again at Los Alamos, but as a civilian. He must have been with his mother more, since in 1948 she mentions in her desk diary that they had gone together the previous year to get a liquor license.[27] Richard probably lived in Frijoles Canyon while he worked at S-Site, a Los Alamos Laboratory research area located less than ten miles from the canyon bottom.

Whatever normality there was to the season ended with Richard's death on September 1, 1947. He died in an Albuquerque hospital after being hospitalized for ten days. His father had joined his mother at the bedside. Richard was twenty-three.

The cause of Richard's untimely death is not generally known. This has given rise to considerable speculation from the public and contradictory statements from his mother. Oral tradition says he had a car accident going to or coming from his work. Fellow workers at Los Alamos claimed that he was part of a group of young men experimentally drinking laboratory alcohol and that he inadvertently poisoned his kidneys.

Mrs. Frey herself, in later years, publicly blamed Richard's death on his participation in the Trinity atomic test explosion.

My young son, Richard, witnessed this. He was twenty-two and had taken part in this, which I shall always believe caused his death [from residual effects].[28]

She also blamed his death more generally on his current work at the time.

You know, Richard worked at the lab there and I believe that he was probably contaminated by whatever—working in the lab.[29]

In her desk diary dated April 12, 1948, Mrs. Frey expressed a more ambiguous judgment.

'I go to Albuquerque today to get our liquor license—what a memory. Dick went with me last year—in such high spirits—it was his downfall. We both wished that liquor was never created. How lost I am today without his loving care.'[30]

Richard's death was devastating to his mother, an experience she would never completely come to terms with. Her inscriptions on pictures of Richard are revealing. She wrote these several years later, no doubt as she was going through the photos and reliving those years. Written on a picture of her and a three- or four- year-old Richard in the snow is this example:

'My precious son, was always so loving—I too 'passed' when he died. Loneliness now how dreadful alone.'[31]

From Mrs. Frey's desk diary, April 23, 1949,

'It takes all the courage and fortitude that I can get together to open here—my life and ambition with all incentive lies buried with my fine son. For reasons, I do not feel that I'll be here another year. Living among dead memories has about finished me off. All night long I awaken shaken with grief. I feel that Richard is so close yet he is forever gone. Death, indeed, is so final. I wish where, why, not knowing which way to turn in my loneliness. I hope above all never to trouble my own people—my parents are too old now for me to pass my grief and sorrow on them. I never will, they should not have worry now and I am not so well physically anymore.'[32]

She absorbed it all and kept Richard alive in her heart. An entry in her desk diary on May 6, 1948, reveals her personal preoccupation.

'Today 23 years ago I came into Frijoles to live. I brought my one [ten] month old son, a beautiful loving son, down on a mule.'[33]

George Maoru, a friend of Mrs. Frey's who met her at Ojo Hot Springs after Richard's death, remembers being at Frijoles Canyon Lodge a year or so after Richard died.

We were sitting in this one room talking, and I noticed that there was paper and wood in the fire-place like somebody was getting ready to light it. I said, 'Oh, that's good. It is cold outside and a fire would be nice.' She said, 'Oh no, Richard put the papers and wood in there and he was going to light the fire, but he didn't have the opportunity.' I said, 'How long are you going to keep torturing yourself? But you know, Mrs. Frey, life's short and it's a shame you have to suffer these feelings every time you come in this room. I think if you would light the fire—it's like a person that's afraid of snakes until they touch one, and they somehow lose their fear.' So she said 'Well, go ahead and light it.' I was stupefied that she would allow me to do that, but I did it very quickly. I lit that fire and we sat there and watched the flames and it seemed like it took a burden off of her.[34]

Evelyn Frey's grief for her son continued for the rest of her life.

7. Life Goes On

Evelyn Frey was working in 1947 and 1948, but the only information we have about it is her diary entry in April concerning the liquor license. An entry on October 18, 1949, has her spending time at Ojo Caliente taking the mineral baths to help heal an ankle.

By 1949 she was back on keel professionally. She had hired a chef and his wife, and on May 4 she took $500 from her personal account to pay bills for the hotel. On May 5 she served a group of three hundred people a buffet-style dinner.

As always, traveling to Bandelier was somewhat hazardous. Much of the road from the "Y," where current State Roads 4 and 502 join, was unpaved and grading was sporadic. In 1950 Mrs. Frey wrote to New Mexico Senator Dennis Chavez requesting, among other things, that this road be paved. In 1951 the state paved that portion of the road passing the monument's entrance station and connecting two Los Alamos Laboratory sites, West Gate and Technical Area 33. Still, the road into the park remained graveled up to the final curve into the canyon. Pavement began here, at the Sandoval county line, and continued the quarter of a mile into the parking lot.

Even with the roads as they were, visitors in the period 1945 to 1950 increased almost fivefold, from 9,312 to 45,524 per year. Half came from surrounding communities for daytime visits, especially for picnics in the campground. This use directly clashed with campers, who generally came from far away and were the intended campground occupants. The clash between daytime and overnight use would continue until Bandelier was extended north to State Road 4 in 1961 and the campground was moved to the mesa top in the fall of 1963.

During the ever busier summers, Mrs. Frey's world revolved around her work. She continued to have adventures with chefs.

One summer I had thirteen chefs, maybe not all chefs but I hired them as chefs. But I had thirteen, and most of them were half-drunk all the time. I had to have the serving plate look right and taste right, so I

55

*lived in the kitchen. I'd be up in the rooms—maybe the girl hadn't
come in [and] I had to make bedrooms—run down to the kitchen,
the chef was leaving or—oh, my. But I think I just got too old and
too tired. I decided one time when I was cleaning out those big
refrigerators (I had three) and in the back I found things that should
have been emptied about a week or two before. And I thought, 'Now
Mrs. Frey, don't spend your life cleaning out refrigerators.'*

*. . . I wasn't easy to work with in the kitchen. I was kind of
rough. But one morning, I . . . phoned into Denver and told them I
was desperate. I had no first cook; I had no second cook. They had
exactly what I wanted. I said, 'You get them on the bus and get them
in here.' So I dashed into Santa Fe to pick up this man and his wife,
and for some reason or other the next morning I allowed I better go
down and look at that kitchen kind of early. And I went down and I
waited a little while; there was no one in the kitchen. I went up and
knocked at their door and no one answered, and I opened the door
and went in. And he was lying on the floor dead drunk and she was
in the bed. There was my big bottles of vanilla and my flavoring on
the floor. They drank it all, don't you see? So they said would I take
them back to pay their way to Denver. And I said, 'I'll take you back
to Santa Fe and dump you!' So I did. They never cooked a meal.*

*Now, I have experience like that—don't blame a chef much for
getting drunk because they had to cook a good deal. And they
[customers] gave me about three orders and I'd say, 'No more, now.'*

Even in the ordinary run of things, managing the dining room and two
coffee shops involved a lot of oversight.

*Well, sometime I had five girls waiting in the dining room and the
two coffee shops, and I had a dish washer, then two, and a second
and first cook, and housekeepers. Sometimes I'd have ten or fifteen.
Just the season, the busy season. We always would say, 'Well, Labor
Day's over, now we're going to rest,' don't you see ? . . . I would have
a few young Indian girls and boys, and I just enjoyed them working
so much. And when they wore their little native dresses they would
get beautiful tips. They just all thought they were getting rich right
there, and they about did too. It was nice to work with them. We
haven't enough of them in here working [now].*

When Evelyn Frey moved into the new lodge in 1939, she had decorated the rooms with authentic southwestern craftwork. This was placed in storage when the army took over during World War II. We can only imagine what a joy it must have been for her to once again put out beautiful Navajo rugs and western paintings in the cabins and display Indian pottery, jewelry, and baskets in the gift shop. Southwest art was valuable, however, and did not always stay put.

And at that time—well, I know the maid used to say to me, 'Did you take the little—there was a small Navajo rug—'did you take the rugs off the floor?' and I said, 'Well, no, I didn't have any business taking the rugs off the floor.' 'They're gone, Mrs. Frey.' We couldn't keep authentic Navajo rugs on the floor. They didn't all go away, but a good many did. I hated that, too. . . . I had different artists staying with me here, and now and then maybe they'd leave me a picture for their bill or something like that. And the pictures would go away too.

Mrs. Frey's small gift shop had a wonderful Native American selection that included pottery from Maria Martinez and other San Ildefonso potters, pottery and jewelry from Santo Domingo artisans, and rugs from Navajo weavers. The gift shop, which she ran until 1978 with the later help of her brother Hugh's wife Velma, conveyed the ambience of an old trading post. Much of the merchandise was of museum quality. Mrs. Frey owned many items that she didn't really want to sell but wanted to display. She priced these very high and put them on the harder-to-see topmost shelves. She had accumulated a large supply of authentic goods over the years, and these were what she was now selling.

I must have had—oh, I don't know how many—Germantown [early Navajo rugs]. I think they began to use the Germantown about 1870 something, if I recall this, and also the borders started in around 18- and 70- some-odd. . . . The Germantown yarn was hard to get ahold of and very expensive, and this couple came in here and I didn't—I hadn't been studying the yarn market. I was trying to sell what I had, so they bought most of my Germantown and they're still coming back. And now, the good blankets—I used to put them right on the floor and just give them a real good using—now the good ones you put on the wall and take very good care of them.

In the old lodge, firewood was a precious and very necessary commodity, providing the only source of heat in the winter and the only cooking fuel year around. In the new lodge, firewood was still needed—but now only for each cabin's pueblo-style corner fireplace and for fireplaces in the visitor's center, dining room, and lobby. The fireplaces were very attractive, a central point of charm in any room. To keep them going still took a lot of wood.

When I operated this place here, I had twenty seven fireplaces. And I know I had one man that used to come down from Los Alamos, and he told me frankly one morning, the man kept saying, 'Well, I'm having to take wood to this room in the night.' And I said, 'Well, what's wrong here?' and he said, 'Well, I don't know.' So I asked him [again, and] he said, 'Lady, I come down here to burn the fireplace all night,' and he sat up all night and watched it. So I told him, 'The next time you come in I'm not going to register you in,' but I did. That's right.

Mrs. Frey stockpiled her wood supply. Once, when she was old, a cloudburst on the mesa top created enough run-off from the cliffs to wash her woodpile into the Rito de los Frijoles and on down to the Rio Grande.

That [wood supply] was something to keep going. And I filled this little space right there with firewood; I brought in a couple of men. And we had a flood in here in—oh, I think I've forgotten what year that was—but it came just to the edge of that window over there, and so they had to come over and open the door; it opened inside, I couldn't do a thing with it. So the Park Service chopped the door down and in so doing my woodpile went right on out the door, and I suppose down to Cochiti—got there down in the river. I had no wood—I think [just]a few pieces around.

The old lodge and the new lodge both kept saddle horses that guests could rent for rides. Mrs. Frey stabled her horses down-canyon from the visitor's center in the stables built by the CCC. She had insisted at the time of construction that an apartment be included in the stables and that the Kohler bathroom fixtures from the old lodge be put into the apartment. At some point in the late 1940s, Mrs. Frey contracted out the horse rental, but the concession itself was not discontinued until the mid-1950s. Now only Park Service horses are kept at the stable.

The CCC men landscaped around the monument buildings before they left. Even so, Mrs. Frey added touches to her concession area and to the common spaces in the cabin area. She planted flowers on the slopes. Despite her care, the plants were not without some natural risk.

> We have gophers, believe me, an awful lot of ground [pocket] gophers every place. They come in and take the garden down. I was sitting up one evening over in the cabins and there was an iris in blossom, and we were talking with guests up there [about] how lovely the iris was. Why, [while] we looked at it—it went right down the hole! They're ground gophers, and as far as I know, they never die. We just have them all over everywhere.

In the early 1950s Meyer Berger of the *New York Times* wrote to Mrs. Frey again with the same offer to write her story for the newspaper. Berger was now a well known editor and Pulitzer Prize winner. Mrs. Frey still didn't take up his offer, although she did keep in touch with him.

During the yearly off season, generally October or November through April, Mrs. Frey would travel, take a room at the La Fonda Hotel in Santa Fe, or rent an apartment in Albuquerque. According to her friend George Maoru,

> Mrs. Frey, after she closed the lodge, would take her vacation—I believe she had some relatives in the south—and after she came back from vacation, she would come up to Ojo Caliente and stay from one to two weeks, where she would take the mineral baths and sort of relax. And then she would live at the La Fonda Hotel in Santa Fe at that time, and she would—after taking, of course, the baths—she would make preparations to open up the lodge in the spring. One

year I had the opportunity to assist her with that. [By then] she didn't drive, so she always came—somebody always brought her up to the springs or she came up on the bus and somebody would always take her back down to Santa Fe.[35]

(In her later years Mrs. Frey had owned a 1962 white Ford Falcon station wagon with cattle-brand-imprint seat covers. Having a car and the independence it brought were very important to her. Canyon people knew when she was leaving by the sound of the car and the way she drove—a way politely termed rakish. Mrs. Frey finally gave up driving in the early 1980s when she was nearly ninety. Her hearing and eyesight were failing and she was afraid she might hit a child.)

Travel to Frijoles Canyon was definitely increasing. Thousands of visitors were overwhelming Bandelier facilities, which had not been constructed to accommodate such numbers. At the same time, an enlarged park staff needed additional office space. The two worst site conditions contributing to the overcrowding were the cramped canyon floor and the space occupied by the campground.

The proposed solution was to relocate the campground and possibly other canyon facilities away from the area. To that end, the Park Service acquired Frijoles Mesa, just north of Frijoles Canyon, in 1961. Construction of an overnight campground on the mesa began in 1963. The old campground in the canyon became a designated picnic area for daytime use only. It reasonably followed that overnight accommodations in the form of the lodge cabins should be eliminated eventually. Mrs. Frey recognized that the lodge was being phased out and wrote about it in her diary.[36]

In 1964 she wrote that Hugh and Velma were helping but cabin reservations were few. She could see that short orders for hamburgers, hot dogs, and the like were the direction that food service was headed and she was considering turning the dining room into a large coffee shop for short orders. She had a soft drink machine, but it didn't make much money—only ten cents on the dollar. She said she couldn't get good

Navajo rugs anymore, although she did sell a Two Gray Hills. She raised the daily cabin rates by $1.00, but it was still not a good season. Her auditor told her, she said, that she was going too far into the red.

In 1965 she wrote that her small grocery stock had not sold well since the campground was moved to the mesa top and gasoline would no longer be sold in the canyon. She said that her cabin prices were lower than those at other resorts. She put an ad in the *Santa Fe New Mexican* and sent out fifteen hundred postcards to advertise her rates. Wood for the fireplaces was expensive and she installed natural gas in six of the cabins. She said she depended on Hugh and Velma.

> May 1965: *I am just plain tired, I guess, and at this stage easily discouraged after 40 years of trying.*
> June 1965: *I have known for four years that there's little use for a dining room—even what guests there are go over to the campground and cook, a lot out of cans.*
> September 1965: *I'm real tired—just can't do my share of work anymore. Arthritis has been quite severe in my neck now for a couple of weeks. Will go to Ojo for water and baths after we close.*

In 1966 Hugh and Velma were helping again. Mrs. Frey drew the $2,000 it took to open from her personal account.

> May 1966: *A $1.00 NPS charge* [probably a monument entrance fee] *really finished my Los Alamos lunch business.*
> June 1966: *Very poor curio shop sales. I am pretty low.*

Sales were off nearly $5,000 in 1967.

> Summer? 1967: *I hope to go through this and next season and at least have enough saved for the time when I can't do for myself. This evidently won't be too long now as I find I am truly tired and can't find a thing to hold to. The NPS simply don't care whether I make a living—even cut my menu down, when all food is rising—O'me!!! I do indeed wonder at times, what is it all about—there is a reason—but I can't find it yet.*
> September 1967: *I was glad to close this year early. All were weary and [I] also was disgusted.*
> September 1967: *There are many proposed changes now here.*

This is because the lease runs out in '69 and I'm getting <u>OLD</u>. No one has any use for us in old age and I simply feel I'm not up to doing the hard work I am expected to do now. Anyway '68 will be another way of life for me as I will be expected to make concession changes. I really do not have much choice as the time arrives for me to either stay here [or leave] and since I've spent my best years here—also done my best work—I will want to remain here. Here I had my happiest days and my greatest sorrow. 1968 is the year of my change for better? or worse. <u>I do not</u> know.

Well-known people continued to visit the monument. Some were routinely mentioned in the monthly report, but many of the most interesting did not warrant such attention. Mrs. Frey specifically remembered one visitor.

This old lady [was] sitting on our portal, and the group that she was with were able to walk, and she wasn't, so she was waiting for them to go through the ruins. So I gave her a cup of tea or coffee, I've forgotten which, and I think I visited with her a little. But in six months I received a letter from Calcutta, India—from our consul thanking me for having served his auntie a cup of tea. So much for little things, don't you see? And he later came to visit here. Very nice gentleman, too. And I thought, that was quite a lot to happen with handing an elderly woman a cup of tea.

During this period Mrs. Frey lost three close family members—her father in 1956 and both her brothers, Jack and Hugh, in 1971. Her ex-husband George died December 31, 1966.

In February 1975 Evelyn Frey turned eighty-three years old.

8. The Last Years

On May 5, 1925, George, Evelyn, and Richard Frey had entered Frijoles Canyon on foot. Fifty years later, Mrs. Frey was still in the canyon as a concessionaire. New Mexico paid tribute to her with a "Mrs. Evelyn Frey Day." The Bandelier Superintendent's Annual Report for 1975 stated,

> On May 3, 1975 the 50th anniversary of Mrs. Frey's life in the canyon was celebrated with a pot luck supper and a preview of the new museum. Mrs. Frey is one of the concessioners at Bandelier and her life is part of the history of the park.[37]

The Southwest Regional Director of the National Park Service, Joseph C. Rumburg, spoke. He acknowledged Mrs. Frey's fifty years as a concessionaire and stated that she had served under every national director of the Park Service. Her presence in Bandelier, he said, was one reason it was such a special place.

Thus began a series of recognitions for Mrs. Frey's accomplishments in Frijoles Canyon—expressions of wonder for a way of life that was past and delight at hearing her bring this period to life. Articles appeared in the *Albuquerque Journal,* the *New Mexican Magazine,* the *Empire Magazine* of the *Denver Post,* the *Santa Fean,* the *Santa Fe New Mexican,* and the *Los Alamos Monitor.* She became a tourist attraction herself as people came to see and speak with "Mrs. Frijoles."

Mrs. Frey was also recognized away from the monument.

> *And I meet them [the CCC workers] as yet once in a while on the street. I met one not long ago and he touched my shoulder and asked me if I was Mrs. Frey, and I said, 'Yes,' and he said that [these were] his grandkids—I think they were this high. I said, 'How did you know me?' and he said, 'I knew your hair.' I've always had bangs, I guess.*

As the years progressed, she never allowed her hair to "go gray" but dyed it herself using dark-red Loving Care hair color. She favored shirtwaist dresses (never wore slacks), red lipstick, and Loving Care face powder. She wore her glasses on a chain around her neck.

The last six lodge cabins closed in the autumn of 1976. At the end of the year Mrs. Frey turned them over to monument administration. Frijoles Canyon Lodge was no more. Ironically, in the spring of 1976 the Park Service rehabilitated the old orchard. To retain water rights to the Rito de los Frijoles, park personnel channeled water back into the irigation ditch feeeding the orchard and planted fruit trees in the orchard site. Manyof the new trees didn't survive because canyon deer found them delicious, but several of the old original apple trees continue to do well today.

Mrs. Frey continued as concessionaire for the gift shop but found it increasingly difficult to stock merchandise of the quality she wanted and sell it at a profit. In December 1978 she requested that the National Park Service let her close the gift shop permanently because it couldn't support itself. The monument superintendent's annual report for that year announced,

> All concession permits expired at the end of December. The snack
> bar operator as well as the curio shop operator, Evelyn C.Frey,
> indicated they were either not interested or no longer able to continue
> their business activities.[38]

For some time the snack bar had been run by a long-time Santa Fe business, Bert's Burger Bowl, owned by good friends Bert and Emma Bertram. Bert and Emma's time at the monument snack bar is especially remembered for its chili dogs, hamburgers, chili stews, and breakfasts. Bert's Burger Bowl is still in business on Guadalupe Street in Santa Fe.

For Mrs. Frey, termination of concessionaire responsibility after all those years was a relief.

> *I gave up my shop last December [1978]. I was the oldest*
> *continual, or continuous I think is a better word, concessionaire in*
> *the Park Service. I had been here fifty four years. But it got to be a*
> *little trying. I think I was a little weary and maybe just a little*

*indifferent—I don't know—I didn't want to be. But I was weary,
anyhow.*

Mrs. Frey closed out her Frijoles Canyon Lodge business bank
account in April 1979.

The Southwest Parks and Monuments Association (SPMA) runs the
bookstores at most Park Service areas in the southwest. Realizing that
Mrs. Frey was an asset, Bandelier requested a $4,500 donation from
SPMA to hire her as a sales clerk for the 1979 summer season. The
money was delightedly provided by Earl Jackson, long-time SPMA head
and a former superintendent of Bandelier. He exhorted Mrs. Frey to
agree to be interviewed and recorded. Years before, Mrs. Frey had
taken Jackson—young, single, and in his first job with the National Park
Service—under her wing and kept him fed. She had been asked several
times to make oral tapes of her remembrances but, with the exception of
a talk she gave to the Los Alamos Historical Society docents in 1975 and
one with Peggy Pond Church to the Los Alamos Historical Society in
1980, she "would not hear of it." Now, however, she was very cooperative.

On May 7, 1979, Evelyn Frey joined the SPMA as a summer book
sales clerk in the visitor's center, working Monday through Friday from
10:00 a.m. to mid afternoon. A day or two before she was to start, she
let Chris Judson, the visitor's center supervisory ranger, know, "I haven't
had a boss in fifty years!" But she and Judson, good friends, found it easy
to work with each other. Over the remaining years, Mrs. Frey worked
with several supervisory rangers, calling each "boss lady" or "little boss
lady."

By the time Mrs. Frey began working in the visitor center, she had to
wear a hearing aid. When the hearing aid was out of adjustment, it made
a screech resembling the squeal of the cash register when it required
clearing. Both occurred fairly regularly. This led to a "Mrs. Frey check"
each morning. At the same time that the Park Service staff checked the
hearing aid, they would make sure that Mrs. Frey was as neat and tidy as
she always wanted to be. Her eyesight didn't always allow her to see

face powder on her glasses or dress, and the glasses chain she wore around her neck would often catch the powder.

Each morning someone from the visitor center would go to Mrs. Frey's apartment, clang the cowbell/doorbell, and say, "Mrs. Frey, Mrs. Frey." When she came to the door Mrs. Frey would say, "Hello, dear, are we busy?" Then she would be escorted to work in the visitor's center. Although her job title was sales clerk, her most valuable work was sharing her knowledge and her memories with visitors.

Popular programs called *Visits with Mrs. Frey* were scheduled twice a week. Mrs. Frey never wanted to do them, but once started she would easily talk nonstop for forty-five minutes, taking obvious pleasure in it. Accompanied by a park ranger, she would sit in the gift-shop patio answering questions about her time in the canyon. Her taped words form the backbone of this book.

At the end of Mrs. Frey's workday, which was about four hours long, someone from the visitor's center would walk her back to her home. One afternoon she was just gone—no one knew where. It turned out that when she got ready to leave everyone was busy. So she asked one of the young men in the fire crew to walk her home. She later told the young Park Service women that if they got canes, the young men would walk them home too. She was a romantic.

Mrs. Frey had a genuine concern for all of the "Bandelier family." She loaned money to those needing a "tide-over." She asked about the workers' children and loved to have them visit her. She always had baked goods to share. An understanding and compassionate listener, she helped many people get past hard times in their lives. Although she would never criticize anyone's actions, and in fact would never say anything bad about anyone, she would not hesitate to express her view of a situation. She definitely served as a parent figure for many.

During the time that the dining room/snack bar area still functioned in the present administration building, it became an after-hours gathering place for park workers and some visitors. People would gather on the patio below Mrs. Frey's apartment, get refreshments from the snack bar before it closed, play music, dance, and generally relax. Often lodge guests and park campers would join in and provide some of the entertainment. These were friendly good times. As long as her health and age permitted, Mrs. Frey occasionally came down to the gatherings. She enjoyed them but admonished everyone, especially those with children, not to stay too late or drink too much.

One of Mrs. Frey's hobbies came to light in her later years—an interest in palmistry. Apparently she studied the art of reading palms and became quite good at it, at least quite convincing. Several young rangers whose palms she read marveled at her accuracy.

Evelyn Frey loved nature and especially appreciated the change of seasons. She walked in the canyon at every opportunity, enjoying the flowers and the foliage. Frijoles Canyon is lovely in all the seasons, but Mrs. Frey particularly liked the color of spring leaves; she called that color "apple green." She was also taken with the colorful autumn leaves. On infrequent occasions when someone cleaned for her, leaves could be found under the rug where she was pressing them. Even when she visited other places she would bring home leaves, occasionally having her clothes sent separately because she needed the suitcases for the leaves.

In 1980 Bandelier National Monument celebrated the centennial anniversary of Adolph Bandelier's arrival in the canyon. According to the monument superintendent's annual report for that year,

On the 100th anniversary of Adolph Bandelier's arrival in Frijoles Canyon, Oct. 23, 1880, a mini-lecture series was held at Fuller Lodge in Los Alamos in conjunction with the Los Alamos Historical Society. The three Thursday evenings in October leading up to October 23 featured Charlie Steen speaking on Archeology of the Pajarito Plateau, Dan Murphy on Adolph Bandelier, and Peggy Pond Church and Evelyn Frey on Early Days in the Bandelier Area. Good crowds were present for all three lectures and they were all well received.[39]

On February 20, 1982, eight days after her ninetieth birthday, Mrs. Frey recorded in her desk diary,

Today, among a small flight of sand-hill cranes going north, was a snow white hooper [whooping] crane.[40]

Other entries in her desk diary of that year tell us that she joined the American Association of Retired Persons, paid $25 a month rent in Bandelier, had arthritis and it was a nuisance; she noted that her high blood pressure was bothering her. During this period, no doubt she went back over her pictures and the other mementos of a lifetime. She also prepared a living will. A comment that she put on the back of a page of her hotel register book from 1926 to 1935 sums up her thoughts:

I recall with pleasure having met many of these wonderful people—especially the local folks After Richard's passing I studied religious subjects steadily—never joining a church. I know this, however, it is the way. Then I worked on New Mexico history, many subjects. I accomplished very little, as I see it. Anyway these were very interesting years and I hope I helped those who visited Frijoles Canyon Ranch.[41]

When Mrs. Frey closed her shop in 1978, she still had inventory. In 1982 she held an auction in Santa Fe to liquidate her holdings. According to the Bandelier superintendent's annual report,

Mrs. Evelyn Frey continues in good health and still resides in her house behind the concession facilities. She has been employed during the summer as a sales person for Southwest Parks and Monuments Association since her retirement from the concession operation in1978. Early this year she had an auction and sold most of the high-value rugs, pots and other items that remained in her inventory from her curio shop plus some from her personal collection.[42]

(The little girl in the present museum display is wearing moccasins purchased at this auction by Bandelier ranger Chris Judson.)

In 1986 Mrs. Frey's former Pajarito Plateau neighbor and long-time friend Peggy Pond Church took her own life in Santa Fe. Peggy Pond

Church was younger than Evelyn Frey but had felt herself failing and believed a person should control her own destiny. Mrs. Frey kept the large article from the newspaper chronicling Church's life and death. This was one more, of many a good friend, gone.

The SPMA gives awards each year in several categories. In 1987 Bandelier National Monument received the superior performance award, which is presented at the Tucson home office. Park officials flew to and from Tucson, while the superintendent's wife, Ardis Hunter, and Mrs. Frey drove. Wanting to do a little sightseeing on the way back, they stopped at the Grand Canyon and proceeded home through Farmington, New Mexico. There they had a car accident. Mrs. Frey was hospitalized for a week in Farmington. Her injuries included broken ribs. Although her life wasn't threatened, her age prevented her from bouncing competely back.

Mrs. Frey now moved slower, needed more assistance, and had a live-in helper for awhile. She fell one day in the monument parking lot and broke a wrist, further decreasing her strength and mobility. Although she continued to live alone in her apartment at Bandelier, the staff looked closely after her.

On the morning of September 11, 1988, a Southwest Parks and Monuments employee went to pick her up as usual. The door was locked and there was no answer to her knock. A ranger and maintenance person were summoned and entered the apartment. Evelyn Frey had died of natural causes sometime in the night. She was ninety-six years old.

On September 28, 1988, the Park Service held a memorial service for Mrs. Frey near the old ranch site attended by park staff, friends, and her sister Jane and Jane's husband. The program was simple and touching. Afterward, flowers were placed where the old lodge had been, the site of her happiest times in Frijoles Canyon. Some consideration was given to burying her in Bandelier, but she had arranged years before to be near Richard. Evelyn Frey is buried at Sunset Memorial Park in Albuquerque alongside her mother and her son.

9. Reflections

A life well spent is it's own epitaph.

Evelyn Frey's Thoughts

Many of the stories recorded in Evelyn Frey's oral tapes are duplicated. However, a phrase occasionally stands out and gives insight into her deeper thoughts.

On her life at the old lodge:
In all, it has been a very happy experience to help people enjoy what we had here; mostly the scenery, the food, the horses, and the nice little trips that they did take up. . . . And that has always been my pleasure, to do a little along that line.

On her life in the canyon:
But he [Richard] used to write me. Wherever he'd happen to be, he'd say, 'Oh, Mother, never leave the Frijoles. It's the most beautiful place in the world.'

On where she would go when she was old:
And I said [to Geronima], 'All right, when I get old I don't have anyone to take care of me, but nobody.' And she said, 'Well, you're gonna come and live with me.' So I'm gonna—I've got myself all fixed up.

On the Indian way of life:
They think that when you die, the natural things around you, such as illness, mental or physical, that [if] you have not lived in harmony with the world around you, . . . you have to suffer for it, and this is until you get back in simplicity again. . . . I like their philosophy much better than I do ours. They don't hurry. If they don't get it done today, well, they might not be here tomorrow, so they just take

70

their time and get things done after awhile. . . . I like their
philosophy and like their way of doing business. But we've never
hurried—very much more at the old place. I don't hurry very much
yet.

On change:
Whoever said that nothing remained the same certainly knew their
business.

The world of Evelyn Cecil Frey has never been more beautifully expressed than in this excerpt from "The Rito: Frijoles Canyon," by her friend Peggy Pond Church (used with permission).[43]

I sit here with my old friend remembering years when
the trail to the canyon was narrow. Whoever came here
walked down it as though into another
world or even into
another dimension of time
or of themselves.
Who knows what we sought?
a return to a past not ours?
an escape
a revelation?

What was it that had called us
each one to the sharp brink of this wilderness
and bade us enter here if we were worthy
of time's tranfigurations?
Imagined or real there was something that renewed us
like an ancient wellspring or a legend.

The canyon embraced us as part of its own being;
heard through our ears the ripple cadence of the river,
the mourning dove's slow croon,
the wild turkey's warning

call like a row of struck bells.
Evening till daybreak the stir of invisible creatures,
a rustle, a soft padding, a twig broken,
shadows that fled across moonlight,

moonlight a substance
that spread like a tide, creating islands,
inlets and coves, an archipelago
past which only the stars sailed.

How long ago that was.
The stars retreat farther each year. Human chatter
scrawls jagged lines across the face of silence.
The hew roar now brings thousands
who do not know what roots are
or the seasons of ripening.

"I wonder who else has seen so many changes?"
my old friend sighs, she for whom the canyon
had been home for nearly a lifetime.
We who spent our young days
among the mounds and shards of a vanishing.
What we remember
cannot live after us.
We smile at one another
as though the present were a dream around us.
Within us the canyon and the still melodious river
lead a secret life that only we can enter.

Appendix A

Frijoles Canyon Lodge Guest Register

Over the years many people, famous and otherwise, visited Frijoles Canyon Lodge. The following are a few of the interesting people as they recorded their names in the early lodge register.

A.R. Cecil and his wife; Evelyn Frey's father and stepmother
Hubert Cecil; Evelyn Frey's brother
Jack O. Cecil; Evelyn Frey's brother
Jane Cecil; Evelyn Frey's half-sister
Beatrice Chauvenet; Santa Fe author
Fermor S. Church; master at Los Alamos Ranch School and
      husband of Peggy Pond Church
A. J. Connell; Los Alamos Ranch School Director
Erna Fergusson; Santa Fe author
Edgar L. Hewett; archaeologist who supervised major early
    excavations in Frijoles Canyon and was a founder of the
    Museum of New Mexico
Mrs. Elbert Hubbard; wife of a writer, publisher, and arts
    and crafts movement leader in the east
Mr. and Mrs. J.A. Insley; married in Ceremonial Cave
Charles A. Lummis; author whose lodge ledger note was, "With A.
    Bandelier in 1890 first discovered to the world and to science
    this Tyuoni on Rito de los Frijoles."
H.P. Mera; researcher at the Laboratory of Anthropology and
    noted ethnographer and anthropologist
Peter and Jack Oppenheimer; relatives of J. Robert Oppenheimer
    who would become director of the Los Alamos Laboratory
    during World War II
Caroline C. Pickard; Santa Fe artist whose paintings later hung in the
    lodge cabins

Frank Pinkley; Superintendent of Southwest Monuments
    for the National Park Service, 1923-1940
Ashley Pond; owner of the Los Alamos Ranch School and father
    of author Peggy Pond Church
Will Rogers and his wife; parents of a Los Alamos Ranch School
    student
S. A. Stubbs; researcher at the Laboratory of Anthropology in
    Santa Fe

    In later years, notable visitors were mentioned in the park super-
intendent's annual report. These include the following:

Walter Attwell; engineer for the canyon road
Mrs. Albert Coors, Jr.; wife of the beverage manufacturer
Juan and Rainbird Gonzales; workers in Frijoles Canyon when
    the Lodge of the Ten Elders was constructed and later when
    Dr. Edgar L.Hewett excavated Tyuoni prehistoric pueblo
Mrs. Alice Abbott Gresdale; relative of Judge Abbott and former
    resident of Frijoles Canyon
Mr. and Mrs. Ludovic Kennedy; Mrs. Kennedy was world-famous
    dancer Moira Shearer, who played the lead ballerina in
    The Red Shoes.
Sheila MacDonald; daughter of England's then prime minister, James
    Ramsay MacDonald
Count and Countess Menioca; Naples, Italy
Chuck Richey; landscaper for the Park Service
Chief Evergreen Tree; native of Cochiti Pueblo living in Chicago and
    giving lectures on CBS and NBC radio mentioning Bandelier
    National Monument
William Allan White; Pulitzer Prize-winning journalist

Appendix B

Self-guided Frey Walk
Bandelier National Monument

As you walk the main loop trail in Bandelier National Monument, you will be able to see some remnants of Mrs. Frey's life in Frijoles Canyon.

1. When you leave the back portal of the visitor's center, walk a few paces and look to the left toward the stream. You will see several boulders. Beyond these are the abutments of the first bridge crossing to the campground. When first built, the visitor's center was two buildings connected by an automobile drive-through to the campground. The campground was at the site of the current picnic area.

2. Pause at signpost #3. The cultivated area for the old lodge began here. The area between the path and the creek extending to the big kiva contained cornfields and the chicken shed.

3. At signpost #8 look to the canyon rim on the right. On top of one of the highest cliffs you will see what looks like a lightning rod. This was part of George Frey's radio antenna. The old lodge was directly across the creek; there would have been a similar rod there on the opposite cliff. A wire was strung from one rod to the other and a second wire was dropped to the lodge. Together these wires constituted the radio antenna.

4. The Frey's garden and orchard extended from signpost #8 up-canyon to just beyond signpost #18. As you walk up-canyon, note the large apple trees. These are from the Frey's 1925 planting. The areas with wire fences contain fruit trees planted in 1976. The concrete irrigation ditch is located a few steps to the west. The ditch may have been partially constructed by George Frey, although it was improved by

the monument in 1976. The forest trees have all grown up since the old lodge was closed in 1939.

5. Beyond signpost #18 and halfway to the foot of the stairs ascending to Long House is a sharp bend in the path. This is where George Frey anchored his cable system. He could drive his truck very close to the cable here to facilitate loading and unloading the transport cage. The upper end of the system is marked by a break in the foliage at the top of the cliff.

6. Up-canyon from here were several fields of alfalfa. The ranger cabin was located near Ceremonial Cave and is marked by a large apple tree along the trail.

7. Return to signpost #16 at the bottom of the Frey Trail. This trail, named for Mrs. Frey, is the improved version of the original trail. When the Freys came it was a fairly difficult route. Everything, including guests, had to come down this trail. Subsequently the trail was supplemented by the cable system for supplies and then by the present road in 1933.

8. Return almost to sign post #9 and turn right on the trail towards the Rito. Between this path and Tyuonyi stood a dwelling, perhaps a guest house or hired hand's house. To the left, below Tyuonyi, a saddle room, barn, and cow shed stood close to the stream.

9. Continue across the Rito until you come to a cairn made of tuff. From the old photo here you can determine the location of the old lodge. (Note how much the ponderosa pine to the left of the boulder has grown since the 1925 photo.) The placement of the eight or nine lodge cabins is not easy to determine, and no evidence remains of them today. As you face the cairn, the cabins would have been to your right up-canyon perhaps one hundred yards along the trail. A nearby tree still retains George Frey's iron hitching ring. Look back

at the next big tree. You can see wire around the trunk from the radio antenna; a piece of wire still sticks out of the tree.

10. If you turn right and walk up-canyon on the trail, you may be able to pick out places where horse bridges crossed the Rito.

11. Walk up-canyon until you can get an unobstructed view of the mesa top to the north. You will clearly see a rock shaped like a crouching bear. The rock borders the Frey Trail near where the trail begins its descent into the canyon. This is Bear Rock, used by Mrs. Frey's chef to count the number of guests on their way down expecting lunch.

12. Turn around and continue on the path back to the visitor's center. If you look carefully to the right about one hundred ten to one hundred forty paces beyond the cairn, you will see a fence post nailed to a large ponderosa pine tree. This is a remnant of the fence around a cow lot.

13. Evelyn Frey's living area, beginning in 1939, was located above the current snack bar portal. The door remains and is labeled "private residence." Mrs. Frey had two bedrooms, a kitchen, a bath, and a living room. On both sides of her apartment were small garden areas with fruit trees and flowers. Many monument staff members who helped her in later years still grow plants taken from there. If you look above the portal, you will see the fruit trees as well as the windows (with plants in them) of her living room.

Reference Notes

All of Evelyn Frey's words are in italics. Her words come primarily from a taped series of informal conversations with Bandelier National Monument visitors and staff occurring between the years 1979 and 1988. The program was called *Visits with Mrs. Frey*. The tapes are stored in the monument archives. Quotes from the *Visits* tapes are given without extra attribution. Mrs. Frey's quotes from other sources are attributed. National Park Service comments come primarily from two internal report series, "Southwest Monuments Monthly Reports" (SMMR) and "Bandelier National Monument Superintendent's Annual Reports" (SAR). These quotes are also attributed.

Attributions:
1. Evelyn Frey, talk to Los Alamos Historical Society docents, Los Alamos, New Mexico, October 1, 1975.
2. Charles Lummis, *Land of Poco Tiempo* (New York: Charles Scribners & Sons,1893), p.98.
3. Neil Judd, *Men Met Along the Trail* (Oklahoma City: University of Oklahoma Press, 1968), p.139.
4. George Maoru, interview with ranger Chris Judson, Bandelier National Monument, New Mexico, August 11, 1994.
5. Peggy Pond Church, *House at Otowi Bridge* (Albuquerque: University of New Mexico Press, 1960).
6. Evelyn Frey, October 1, 1975.
7. Evelyn Frey, talk with Peggy Pond Church to Los Alamos Historical Society, Los Alamos, New Mexico, October 23, 1980.
8. " Southwest Monuments Monthly Report," (SMMR) Bandelier National Monument (Santa Fe: National Park Service), June1933.

9. Evelyn Frey, interview with ranger Sari Stein, Bandelier National Monument, New Mexico, September 10, 1979.

10. SMMR, January 1934.

11. SMMR, January 1934.

12. SMMR, June 1934.

13. SMMR, May 1934.

14. SMMR, June 1936.

15. SMMR, May 1939.

16. SMMR, May 1939.

17. SMMR, January 1940.

18. Bandelier National Monument archives, no date.

19. SMMR, November 1939.

20. SMMR, January 1940.

21. SMMR, October 1940.

22. SMMR, November 1940.

23. Evelyn Frey, untitled memo to Bandelier National Monument, January 24, 1941.

24. Richard Frey, letter to Evelyn Frey, April 2, 1942.

25. *Visits with Mrs. Frey*, with Kevin McKibbin, June 1981.

26. SMMR, August 1946.

27. Evelyn Frey, entry in desk diary, April 12, 1948.

28. Evelyn Frey, viewing July 16, 1945, *Santa Fe New Mexican* newspaper clipping about the first atom bomb blast; tape in Bandelier National Monument archives.

29. George Maoru, August 11, 1994.

30. Evelyn Frey, entry in desk diary, April 12, 1948.

31. Evelyn Frey, photos in Bandelier National Monument archives.

32. Evelyn Frey, entry in desk diary, April 23, 1949.

33. Evelyn Frey, entry in desk diary, May 6, 1948.

34. George Maoru, August 11, 1994.

35. George Maoru, August 11, 1994.

36. Evelyn Frey, entries in desk diary, 1964, 1965, 1966, and 1967.
37. "Superintendent's Annual Report," (SAR) Bandelier National Monument (Santa Fe: National Park Service), 1975.
38. SAR, 1978.
39. SAR, 1980.
40. Evelyn Frey, entry in desk diary, February 20, 1982.
41. Frijoles Canyon Lodge Register Book, 1926-1935.
42. SAR, 1982.
43. Peggy Pond Church, "The Rito: Frijoles Canyon," from *Birds of Daybreak: Landscapes and Elegies* (Santa Fe: William Gannon, 1985), p.19.

Bibliography

Abbott, Albert. Letter to his son Roger Abbott dated January 12, 1948. Los Alamos, Bandelier National Monument.

Bandelier National Monument, New Mexico, A Proclamation by the President of the United States. Washington, D.C., 47 Stat 2503, February 5, 1932.

Church, Peggy Pond. *Birds of Daybreak.* Santa Fe: William Gannon, 1985.

_____. *House at Otowi Bridge: The Story of Edith Warner and Los Alamos.* Albuquerque: University of New Mexico Press, 1960.

Curtis, Olga. "Evelyn Frey: She's 'Mrs. Frijoles.' " *Empire Magazine* (17 August 1975): 12.

Daggett, Eleanor. "Queen of the Canyon." *New Mexico Magazine* (May 1977): 33.

Frey, Evelyn. *Visits with Mrs. Frey.* Los Alamos, Bandelier National Monument, oral tapes between 1979 and 1988.

Fry, Marian. "A Lifetime at Bandelier." *Los Alamos Monitor* (23 May 1976).

Goodchild, Peter. *J. Robert Oppenheimer: Shatterer of Worlds.* New York, Fromm International Publishers, 1985.

Harrison, Laura Soulliere, Randall Copeland and Roger Buck. *Historic Structure Report 1988: CCC Buildings, Bandelier National Monmument, New Mexico.* Denver, U.S. Department of the Interior, National Park Service, 1988.

Hatch, Alden. *Remington Arms in American History.* New York, Rinehart and Company, Inc., 1956.

Hendron, J.W. *Frijoles: A Hidden Valley in the New World.* Santa Fe, Rydal Press, Inc., 1946.

Hewett, Edgar L. *The Proposed "National Park of the Cliff Cities."* Papers of the School of American Archaeology No. 34. Washington, D.C., Archeological Institute of America, 1916.

Hoard, Dorothy. *Guide to Bandelier National Monument.* Los Alamos, New Mexico, Los Alamos Historical Society, 1989.

——————. *Los Alamos Outdoors.* Los Alamos, New Mexico, Los Alamos Historical Society, 1993.

Howard, Kathleen L. and Diana F. Pardue. *Inventing the Southwest: The Fred Harvey Company and Native American Art.* Flagstaff, Northland, 1996.

Hunter, Ardis. "Evelyn Frey, Pioneer." *Santa Fean* (September 1979): 10.

Judd, Neil M. *Men Met Along the Trail: Adventures in Archaeology.* Norman, University of Oklahoma Press, 1968.

Kailer, Pat. "Evelyn Frey Day: Bandelier Resident Reminisces About How It Used to Be." *Albuquerque Journal Trends* (4 May 1975).

Kaufman, Polly Watts. *National Parks and the Woman's Voice.* Albuquerque, University of New Mexico Press, 1996.

Lummis, Charles. *Land of Poco Tiempo.* Albuquerque, University of New Mexico Press, 1975 reprint of 1893 publication.

Pack, Arthur Newton. *We Called It Ghost Ranch.* Abiquiu, New Mexico, Ghost Ranch Conference Center, 1965.

Parker, Roscoe S. (Captain, Seventh U.S. Cavalry). 'Bandelier Water Supply,' Letter to Post Quartermaster, Fort Bliss, Texas, December 28, 1933.

Rothman, Hal. *Bandelier National Monument: An Administrative History.* Southwest Cultural Resources Center Professional Papers Number One. Santa Fe, Southwest Cultural Resources Center, 1988.

————. *On Rims and Ridges: The Los Alamos Area Since 1880.* Lincoln, University of Nebraska Press, 1992.

Seidel, Robert W. *Los Alamos and the Development of the Atomic Bomb.* Los Alamos, New Mexico, Otowi Crossing Press, 1995.

Southwest Monuments Monthly Reports, Bandelier National Monument. Santa Fe, National Park Service, 1933-1946.

Southwest Parks Annual Reports, Bandelier National Monument. Santa Fe, National Park Service, 1975-1982.

Taylor, Diane, et.al. *The 1977 LaMesa Fire Study.* Santa Fe, National Park Service, 1990.

Thomas, Diane H. *Southwestern Indian Detours.* Phoenix, Hunter Publishing Company, 1978.

INDEX

1. Evelyn Cecil, Encino, New Mexico ~1916

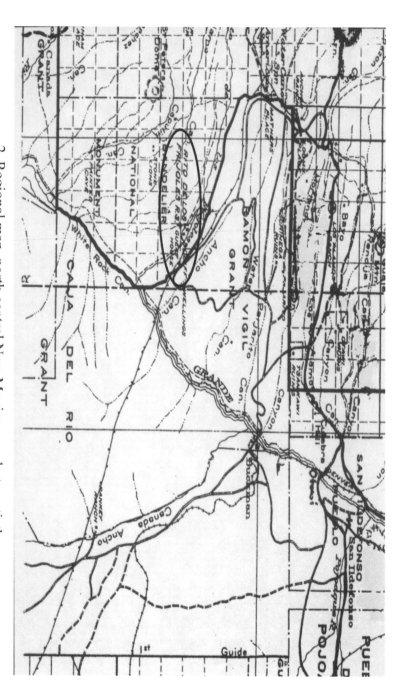

2. Regional map, north central New Mexico—early twentieth

3. Evelyn Frey and baby son Richard—1924 or 1925

4. Frijoles Canyon Lodge—1925

5. Frijoles Canyon Lodge outbuildings dating from
Ten Elders Ranch~1910 (1935 photo)

6. Cliff view into Frijoles Canyon showing Tyonyi ruin and portion of Frey garden area— probably late 1920s

7. United States Forest Service ranger cabin—probably late 1920s

8. George and Richard Frey with dog, Frijoles Canyon—probably late 1920s

9. Evelyn (center), George (far right), and Richard Frey with Reed family, Frijoles Canyon—1930

10. Richard Frey and chickens, Frijoles Canyon—early 1930s

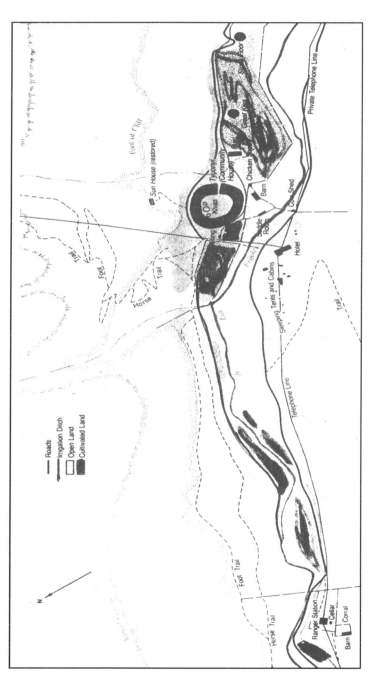

11. Frijoles Canyon ranch building layout—early 1930s. From Hal Rothman. *On Rims and Ridges: The Los Alamos Area Since 1880* (Lincoln: University of Nebraska Press, 1992), p. 194.

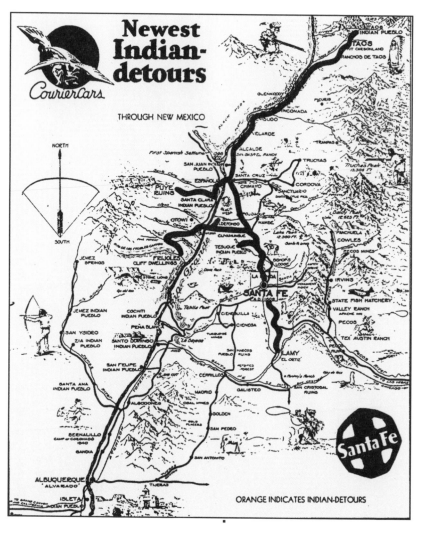

12. Santa Fe Railroad Indian Detours advertisment map—1931

13. Swimming hole during Civilian Conservation Corps days—mid 1930s

She climbs out of a canyon to get The New York Times

ONE of our reporters comes back from an auto trip through the West with an amazing and gratifying story about a woman who thinks The New York Times is a pretty good newspaper. She climbs out of her canyon home every week and makes a long, arduous trip to the nearest trading post to get her copy.

This has been going on for some thirteen years ... ever since she, her invalid husband and their child moved into Frijole Canyon, a deep cut in the mountains of New Mexico where lie the ruins of one of the most ancient of Pueblo cities. When they moved into the canyon, they lowered their supplies on a steel cable and carried in their goods and their baby on a horse they had to lead on foot for miles and miles to the valley floor.

And through it all, they have maintained but one contact with the world outside the canyon — The New York Times. "The Times," they say with touching simplicity, "is our Bible."

... Such reader loyalty humbles us. But it has its practical meaning for you, too. A newspaper that commands such reader devotion (and people everywhere seem to feel pretty much as does our Frijole Canyon friend) must be a force indeed for advertisers to reckon with in its home community. And reckoning with The Times, advertisers find, is the key to complete success in New York.

The New York Times

"ALL THE NEWS THAT'S FIT TO PRINT"

CHICAGO: 230 NORTH MICHIGAN AVE. • BOSTON: BOSTON GLOBE BUILDING • DETROIT: GENERAL MOTORS BUILDING

FEBRUARY 15, 1939

14. *New York Times* advertisement—February 15, 1939

15. Richard Frey—1945. On back of picture, "On furlough to California ..."

16. Lobby at Frijoles Canyon Lodge—probably mid 1950s

17. Patio for Frijoles Canyon Lodge guest houses—probably mid 1950s

18. Coffee shop, Frijoles Canyon Lodge—mid 1950s

19. Mrs. Frey's turkey design on dining room setting, Frijoles
Canyon Lodge—as it looked mid 1950s
(Photo Courtesy of Sari Stein)

20. Evelyn Frey at home, Frijoles Canyon—1966
(Photo Courtesy of Sari Stein)

21. Evelyn Frey in later years—probably mid 1980s